CAMPAIGN 337

CASTAGNARO 1387

Hawkwood's Great Victory

**KELLY DEVRIES AND
NICCOLÒ CAPPONI**

ILLUSTRATED BY GRAHAM TURNER

Series Editor Marcus Cowper

OSPREY
Bloomsbury Publishing Plc
PO Box 883, Oxford, OX1 9PL, UK
1385 Broadway, 5th Floor, New York, NY 10018, USA
E-mail: info@ospreypublishing.com
www.ospreypublishing.com

OSPREY is a trademark of Osprey Publishing Ltd

First published in Great Britain in 2019

A catalogue record for this book is available from the British Library.

ISBN: PB 9781472833518; eBook 9781472833563; ePDF 9781472833570; XML 9781472833587

19 20 21 22 23 10 9 8 7 6 5 4 3 2 1

Maps by Bounford.com
3D BEVs by The Black Spot
Index by Alan Rutter
Typeset by PDQ Digital Media Solutions, Bungay, UK
Printed in China through World Print Ltd.

DEDICATION

For Gian Annibale 'Pucci' Rossi di Medelana, whose admiration for Sir John Hawkwood is unbounded.

ACKONWLEDGEMENTS

Maria Pertile, for her translation from the Venetian; the staff of the Archivio di Stato di Lucca; Dr Marco Morin; Dr Mary V. Davidson; Dr Ciro Paoletti; Messer Franco Sacchetti; Professor William J. Connell; Dr Marcello Simonetta; Dr Michael Livingston; Robert Woosnam-Savage, Kay Smith; Ruth Rhynas Brown; the Royal Armouries, United Kingdom, and Loyola College of Arts and Science, Loyola University Maryland.

ARTIST'S NOTE

Readers may care to note that the original paintings from which the color plates in this book were prepared are available for private sale. All reproduction copyright whatsoever is retained by the publishers. All enquiries should be addressed to:

Graham Turner, PO Box 568, Aylesbury, Bucks, HP17 8EX, UK
www.studio88.co.uk

The publishers regret that they can enter into no correspondence upon this matter.

Osprey Publishing supports the Woodland Trust, the UK's leading woodland conservation charity. Between 2014 and 2018 our donations are being spent on their Centenary Woods project in the UK.

To find out more about our authors and books, visit **www.ospreypublishing.com**. Here you will find extracts, author interviews, details of forthcoming events and the option to sign up for our newsletter.

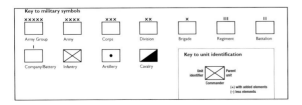

Sir John Hawkwood was the most famous mercenary captain in medieval Europe. He learned his craft fighting for England during the early Hundred Years War in France. After 1360, when peace brought wages to an end, he joined other soldiers fighting in Italy, initially for the famous White Company. He quickly rose to leadership, primarily in the hire of Florence, justifiably honoured in his death by a fresco painted by Paulo Uccello on the wall of the Duomo, from which this detail is taken. (Photo by © Alinari Archives/CORBIS/Corbis via Getty Images)

CONTENTS

Italy around 1370

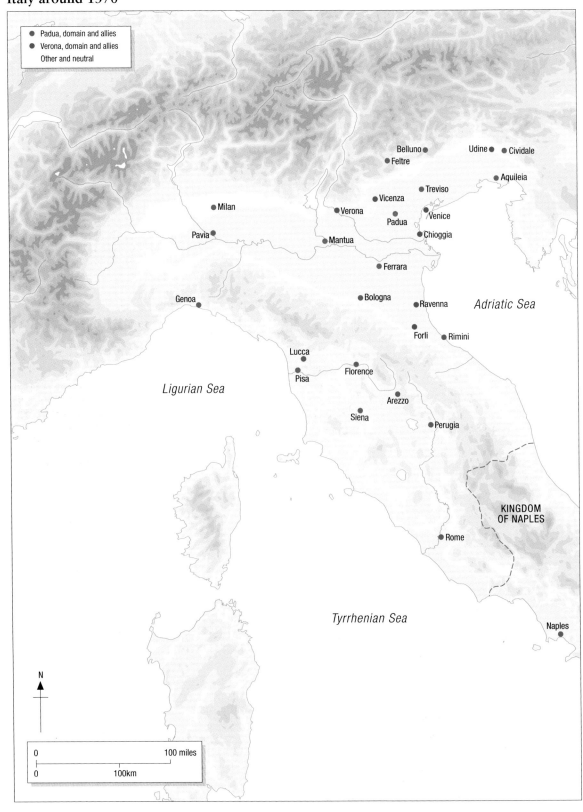

Padua, domain and allies
Verona, domain and allies
Other and neutral

Belluno
Feltre
Udine
Cividale
Aquileia
Treviso
Vicenza
Verona
Venice
Padua
Milan
Chioggia
Pavia
Mantua
Ferrara
Genoa
Bologna
Ravenna
Adriatic Sea
Forli
Rimini
Lucca
Pisa
Florence
Ligurian Sea
Arezzo
Siena
Perugia
KINGDOM
OF NAPLES
Rome
Tyrrhenian Sea
Naples

N

0   100 miles
0   100km

INTRODUCTION

With the rise of the northern Italian towns in the 11th and 12th centuries into separate and, to them, largely sovereign political entities, Italians have seen power as being held rather than bestowed by law, with legal and/or ideological veneers serving as useful props to sustain and uphold authority. By the mid-14th century this had become the accepted state of affairs: Italian Communes, with the notable exception of Venice, having fallen under the sway of – or, at least, having had a brush with – seigniorial rule, dictatorships using the 'fig leaf' of Communal institutions to hide the 'nudity' of their legal justification. As the various political communities – city-states, kingdoms, lordships – struggled for hegemony, in one region or area, military affairs became increasingly entwined with politics and economics. Mercenary companies were by now active and often independent players on the multifaceted international chessboard. The battle of Castagnaro, fought between Padua and Verona on 11 March 1387, was but the outcome of a prolonged chess match with multiple players.

The battle of Castagnaro (or, to be precise, of *the* Castagnaro – the name deriving from a field fortification called after a now-defunct branch of the river Adige) is one of the few Italian medieval fights possessing some name recognition in the English-speaking world. The reason is not difficult to fathom: one of the victors – the principal one, according to many historians – happened to be the renowned English mercenary captain Sir John Hawkwood. It is easy for us to dub Castagnaro Hawkwood's masterpiece; it is interesting to note that Sir John's contemporaries considered his fighting retreat from the river Adda in 1391, keeping his army together in the process, a far greater success. We tend to consider 'battle' as something skilled military leaders actively sought at all times in the world's history, although in the 14th century an able commander did everything possible to avoid field encounters, wishing not to risk his men, money, equipment and reputation in an always-perilous clash of arms. Castagnaro

This illumination from the *Queste de Saint Graal* made in Milan, shows Percival dressed in a combination of plate and mail armour, with a visored bascinet (the visor raised to allow better sight when not in combat) attached to a mail aventail. (Bibliotheque nationale de France, Département des manuscrits, Français 343)

happened for political and economic reasons as much as military ones and forced the hand of the Carrara, Padua's ruling lords and Hawkwood's employers at the time.

During the Castagnaro campaign parallel political manoeuvrings by a number of powerful entities mirrored those in the field, although the tactical outcome has overshadowed them. If there is anything like a decisive battle, then Castagnaro deserves such a title, given that in the short and near-short run it caused the end of Verona and Padua as independent city-states, both falling into the hands of the Milanese in the 18 months following the battle. Although Padua recovered its freedom – albeit on Venetian sufferance – soon after, there is no doubt that the ultimate winner at Castagnaro was the lord of Milan Gian Galeazzo Visconti, who skilfully used his Paduan allies as an unwitting tool to weaken Verona, only to betray them once he had taken over that city, by striking a deal with Venice to partition Padua's territory. Italian rulers of the 14th century did not need Machiavelli to learn how to be machiavellian.

These crucial historical events notwithstanding, Hawkwood alone looms large in the modern imagery of Castagnaro. English and American authors – with Italian ones following – bear most of the blame. To this day Italy's developments in warfare during the Middle Ages are perceived by many historians to be, to an extent, backwards when compared to the rest of Europe (whereas the opposite is actually true). Accordingly, Hawkwood, employing a flanking movement akin to the one used by the Black Prince at Poitiers 30 years before, is not just an example of tactical brilliance but also of advanced military knowledge. Namely these authors have decided that Castagnaro was fought in a locality that mirrored that of the English 1356 victory and have savaged contemporary sources in order to prove their point.

This, however, has created another problem: what was the performance of the celebrated longbow at the battle? Palpable is the puzzlement of some historians about why on Italian battlefields the English wonder-weapon did not yield the same results as in France. This question has long since plagued those who try to explain this by arguing that Hawkwood's archers were too few in number to produce a telling effect.

All the above has obscured the real military significance of the Castagnaro. It was a tactical gem, but not for the reasons commonly given; a tribute to Hawkwood's leadership, yet in a manner unexpected, and a vindication of the longbow, if not as the often-believed mass killing machine. Hawkwood was, in fact, a far better leader than given credit, being able to adapt his tactics to take advantage of an opportunity on the battlefield, utilizing all his army, cavalry, infantry and longbowmen, trusting in their training and skill.

Two years before the battle of Castagnaro, Gian Galeazzo Visconti, then lord of Pavia, wrested control of Milan by overthrowing his uncle. Following that he became the 'spider' whose web spanned Northern Italy, catching his allies, the Paduans, as well as the Veronese, who would fight several wars until both were so exhausted that their lands eventually became dominated by Milan and Venice. Gian Galeazzo's arms are found at the Sforza Castle in Milan. (Photo by Fototeca Gilardi/ Getty Images)

THE STRATEGIC BACKGROUND

'WILL YOU WALK INTO MY PARLOUR?' SAID THE SPIDER TO THE FLY

Spiders are known to be patient, cunning and swift, three traits of competent politicians. Late 14th-century Italian ones certainly had a very arachnid style of conducting affairs. In 1387 the lord of Milan, Gian Galeazzo Visconti, was poised to become Italy's top web spinner. His rise to power had been spectacular two years before by devious means – capturing, imprisoning and, presumably, murdering his predecessor and uncle, Bernabò. Double-dealing would become second nature for Gian Galeazzo, as he started weaving threads to accomplish his ultimate goal: to become the ruler of the whole of north and central Italy. To reach this objective Gian Galeazzo would unabashedly use every dirty trick in the Italian political book, betraying his allies time and time again to enlarge his web of power; the nursery rhyme, *The Spider and the Fly*, is uniquely apt in describing the lord of Milan's deeds. Still, if we accept the saying about hypocrisy being a compliment vice pays to virtue, then it is no chance that one of Visconti's favourite titles happened to be the *Count of Virtue* (*Il Conte di Virtù* in Italian; a corruption of *Vertus*, a fief bestowed on the lord of Milan by the king of France).

Gian Galeazzo lost no time inserting himself in the ongoing conflict between Padua and Verona; his objective was to weaken one of the two, if not both, city-states, making them therefore easier to grab. This war was just the most recent episode of a long-standing and widespread power struggle in northern Italy. In the first decades of the 14th century, Verona had been the most powerful player in the area, mainly thanks to the able leadership of the city's lord, Cangrande Della Scala, among his successes the conquest of Padua in 1328. However, under Mastino II, Cangrande's over-ambitious successor, Verona saw its power eroded by widespread rebellions of subject-cities, shifting international alliances, a string of military defeats and Venice starting to take an active interest in the mainland (*la terraferma*) to its west. Padua became one of Mastino's biggest losses: in 1337 the city shook off Veronese domination and accepted Venetian suzerainty. This prohibited Verona's access to strategically important communication routes in the Po Valley. As a result, Cansignorio Della Scala, Mastino's son and heir, opted for a different policy, trying to keep good relations with his neighbours and avoid war as much as possible. Besides, by this time Verona had come to rely on Venice as its main trading partner, as well as a bulwark against others' expansionism, including that of Milan and Padua.

This detail from the Crucifixion Altarpiece from the Chartreuse de Champmol, carved in 1390–99 by Jacques de Baerze and Melchior Broederlam, shows St George dressed in late 14th-century plate cuisses, poleyns and greaves – to cover the legs – and sabatons – to cover the feet. He wears steel gauntlets, the articulated plates attached to his gloves visible. What he wears under his tunic cannot be seen, although as it fits so tightly it is likely a brigandine. The visor of his bascinet, attached to an aventail, is raised, so that unimpeded he can see the dragon as he delivers the killing blow with his sword. (De Agostini/G. Dagli Orti)

By the late 1340s Padua had turned against the Venetians' stifling overlordship, which had created a deep-seated resentment. This was adroitly exploited by Padua's *signore* Francesco 'il Vecchio' da Carrara, who also nourished ambitions – like Gian Galeazzo Visconti – of becoming the paramount power in northern Italy. The Venetians also imposed onerous conditions on Padua in exchange for military aid during the Hungarian-Venetian war of 1356–58, when the troops of Louis I of Hungary started pillaging Paduan territory. As a result, not only did Carrara agree to supply victuals to the Hungarians, but he also provided them with military assistance against Venice. The Venetians would never forget Padua's 'treason', but in the meantime Francesco had earned Louis's long-standing friendship, as well as his written promise to come to Carrara's aid if needed.

The hostility between Padua and Venice simmered during the 1360s. Initially, the conflict was conducted by proxy, the Venetians for instance backing the Archduke of Austria's designs over the Patriarchy of Aquileia, one of Padua's confederates. Francesco reacted by considerably enlarging his alliance network, one of his most significant partners being Florence; indeed, so close was the bond between the two cities, that in 1370 Francesco, his wife and descendants were made Florentine citizens. In the years to come this relationship would prove vital for him.

Open war between Padua and Venice erupted in 1372, after tension had escalated in a series of border clashes followed by commercial retaliations. An attempt by Florence and others of Carrara's allies to mediate between the parties came to naught when Venice discovered a plot by the Paduan lord to assassinate several hostile Venetian politicians. In the autumn of the same year, Paduan forces launched an invasion in the direction of Treviso. Initially successful, the arrival of Venetian reinforcements from the east forced Carrara to retreat, his plight made worse in March 1373 when he uncovered a Venetian-backed conspiracy against him headed by his half-brothers, Marsilio and Nicolò. Hammered on all sides, all help from his allies unable to stem the enemy tide, Carrara was forced to accept a humbling peace the following September. He never forgot nor forgave this humiliation, according to a contemporary chronicle 'staying awake at night, always thinking of a way to avenge himself on the Venetians and damage them in every possible way'.

The chance for revenge came five years later, when Padua joined a powerful anti-Venetian alliance comprising Hungary, the Patriarchy of Aquileia and Genoa. The first year of the war, starting in June 1378, saw these allies successful, Genoese and Paduan troops managing to occupy the isle of Chioggia, 30km south of Venice (and giving the war its name), thus blocking the sea routes into the Lagoon. All Venetian peace overtures were stymied by Francesco's burning opposition to any deal, saying to the Venetian ambassador: 'Go and tell your government that we shall receive no embassy until we have tied our horses at St Mark's palace'. Digs such as this one only stiffened Venice's will to resist, until reinforcements from the eastern Mediterranean turned the tide of the war in its favour. Even so, the 1381 peace treaty was on the whole favourable to Padua, and in the next four years Carrara managed to extend his domains east, capturing Treviso and Udine. Venice was understandably concerned about growing Paduan power and started forging alliances in order to curb Carrara's ambitions, the Veronese being happy to oblige.

Cansignorio Della Scala had died in 1375, leaving as successors his two illegitimate children, Bartolomeo and Antonio. The two brothers, minors at the time of their coming to power, nevertheless successfully repulsed a Milanese invasion of their territories in 1378–79. Bernabò Visconti's excuse for waging war was regaining the possessions of his wife, Beatrice 'Regina' Della Scala, allegedly usurped by her brother Cansignorio. Bernabò would blame his failure on the defection in February 1379 of his two senior commanders, John Hawkwood and Lutz von Landau – incidentally also his sons-in-law, having married two of the lord of Milan's illegitimate daughters. Milanese chroniclers would squarely accuse them of being bribed by the Veronese. Peace between Milan and Verona was negotiated soon after, the Della Scala brothers agreeing to pay Beatrice a substantial indemnity. During the conflict the Veronese had enjoyed the military support of Genoa and Hungary, while Milan had formed an alliance with Venice; thus when the War of Chioggia broke out the same year, the Della Scala brothers, albeit with misgivings, went along with their confederates. The Veronese, despite the recent peace treaty, still considered Bernabò Visconti a major threat. Tensions between Verona and Venice would continue, the two states engaged in a drawn-out struggle over trade issues.

No sooner had the Chioggia War ended than Venice found itself embroiled in another conflict, this time over the succession of the Patriarchy of Aquileia. In 1378 schism had split the Catholic Church, the initial squabble internal to the Papal *curia*, quickly escalating into a political rupture cutting

This painting celebrates Charles III of Durazzo's conquest of Naples in 1381; the detail here showing the new king's triumphal entry into the city. Among the troops who fought besides Charles was John Hawkwood and his mercenary company. Painted around 1400 by an anonymous painter in Florence, it now resides in the Metropolitan Museum of Art. (Photo by Geoffrey Clements/Corbis/VCG via Getty Images)

across the length of Europe. Some states – such as England, Poland, Hungary and the Low Countries – backed the Roman pontiff Urban VI, and others – principally France, Aragon, Castile, Naples and Scotland – the Avignonese Pope Clement VII. Forced to choose between Rome and Avignon, most states in north and central Italy favoured Rome, although were ready to switch sides according to political expediency. In 1382 the Patriarch of Aquileia, Marquard of Randeck, died, in his place Urban VI nominating Cardinal Philippe d'Alençon, cousin of King Charles VI of France. Alençon had been one of those who had brought about the election of Clement, but two years later had reconciled himself with Urban. The cardinal's appointment to the see of Aquileia proved controversial from the start. Local rivalries caused a split within the new patriarch's extensive domains, something Venice was quick to exploit to its advantage. For a while the Republic on the Lagoon had set eyes on Aquileian territories, considered a buffer between Venice and some of its most aggressive neighbours, such as the Archduke of Austria and the King of Hungary. Besides, the Patriarchy of Aquileia had recently become an ally of Padua, Francesco da Carrara coveting the towns of Feltre, Belluno and Treviso, to link his own territories with those of the patriarchy. In addition, although Alençon was in Urban's camp, his connections with the French crown made him suspect to those, for instance, the Venetians, who backed the Roman pontiff.

Further fears of French intervention in Italy were fuelled in 1382 by the news of Bernabò Visconti's negotiations to marry his daughter, Lucia, to the son and namesake of Louis of Anjou, Count of Provence and claimant to the throne of Naples. The kingdom had recently fallen into the hands of Charles of Anjou, the Duke of Durazzo, after the capture and death of Queen Joanna I. She, however, had previously nominated Louis her heir and he now put together an army to win back his rightful inheritance – with the overt help of Charles VI of France and the Avignon papacy, since Charles of Durazzo followed Rome. Louis's descent into Italy was actively supported by Bernabò, less so by Florence and Venice, which, while ostensibly neutral, perceived the expedition as a threat to their interests. Florence, though, was still recovering, from four years of internal turmoil and still struggling to find a consistent foreign policy; Venice, licking its wounds from the Chioggia War and its hands full with the war ravaging the Patriarchy of Aquileia, could do little to stop the French inroad.

Once it reached southern Italy Louis's expedition floundered, hampered by disease, famine and enemy activity. The *condottieri* John Hawkwood, now in Pope Urban's service, and Alberigo da Barbiano, subjected the French to incessant hit-and-run warfare. Desperate, Louis appealed for help to the king of France and Pope Clement, the latter providing money and the former an army under the formidable Enguerrand VII de Coucy. Putting together such a force required time, and it was only in the early summer of 1384 that de Coucy managed to enter Italy, once again with the support of Bernabò Visconti. Yet, de Coucy did not get farther than southern Tuscany, his only exploit the capture of the Durazzo-controlled city of Arezzo, which he promptly sold to Florence for a hefty sum before returning to France on receiving news of Louis's death in September.

Meanwhile, in northern Italy more trouble had been brewing. The attempts of Francesco da Carrara to get Treviso by force had come to naught because of Leopold of Austria's intervention, the Venetians having ceded the city to him during the Chioggia War precisely to avoid it falling into Paduan hands. With all his muscle-flexing, Leopold was not in a financial or military position to maintain his hold on Treviso indefinitely, and therefore preferred to surrender it to Carrara, together with the strongholds of Ceneda and Belluno, for a whopping 100,000 ducats. Carrara entered Treviso in triumph on 4 February 1384 and immediately started pursuing his territorial ambitions in Friuli, Cardinal d'Alençon promising him extensive gains should Francesco manage to pacify the region by subduing the rebellious city of Udine. Carrara's actions caused alarm in Venice, which now found itself nearly surrounded by hostile territories. Consequently, in February 1385 the Republic on the Lagoon formed a league with Alençon's rebellious subjects, managing to draw into it the following May Antonio Della Scala, now sole lord of Verona after murdering his brother four years before. Venice promised Antonio military support against Padua, in exchange for his aiding the rebels in Friuli, although Della Scala was still behaving cautiously. Matters, however, were about to take a dramatic turn.

For some time, Gian Galeazzo Visconti, lord and imperial vicar of Pavia, had been at odds with his uncle Bernabò, who had constantly thwarted his nephew's political schemes. Gian Galeazzo had extensive ties to the French court through his mother and his first wife, which he used to allow himself some freedom of action against the overbearing Bernabò. The latter forced on Gian Galeazzo one of his (legitimate) daughters as a spouse, but he had already pulled off the much more strategically important marriage of his granddaughter, Isabeau of Bavaria, to Charles VI, the king of France. With the looming possibility of being completely sidelined and reduced to a political nullity, possibly also fearing for his life, Gian Galeazzo decided to act.

In early May 1385, Gian Galeazzo informed his uncle that he intended to go on a pilgrimage to the shrine of Santa Maria del Monte, near Varese, and would like to greet him en route. Bernabò, who considered his nephew utterly worthless, suspected nothing when he rode out of Milan the following 6 May, accompanied only by two of his sons; he therefore received a rude shock when finding himself surrounded and taken into custody by Gian Galeazzo's large body of retainers. The coup's organizer swiftly took control of Milan, allowing the citizens to sack his uncle's palace and burn

This kneeling soldier from Altichiero's fresco, *Battle of Clavijo* (1376–79), wears steel plates encasing the front and sides of his legs, although open at the back of the legs and feet, revealing mail beneath. The armour covering his arms is harder to discern, although his steel gauntlets are visible. The soldier's bascinet is attached to an aventail, which appears to be plate, but is more likely mail. A squire is holding a great helm to be placed over the bascinet; on it is a crown meaning that this is King Ramiro I of Asturias, victor of the legendary battle. (Capella di San Giacomo, Padua, Italy/Bridgeman Images)

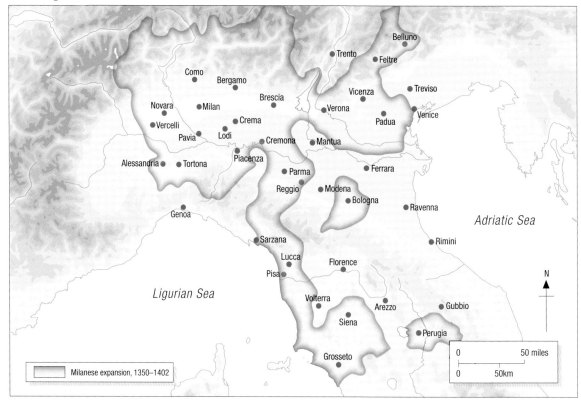

Milanese expansion, 1350–1402

Adriatic Sea

Ligurian Sea

N

0   50 miles

0   50km

OPPOSITE

Although Niccolò Benedetti did not fight in the Veronese–Paduan wars, his effigy, sculpted in 1405 for the Santa Caterina Church in Pisa (and now in the Bardini Museum in Florence), beautifully depicts a knight of the time. Encased in the most expensive plate armour, with the mail worn underneath clearly visible at the back of the knees, waist, upper arms and neck, he nevertheless has chosen to wear the more old-fashioned great helm. Perhaps this was to better hold up the heraldic headpiece shown on the effigy – although bascinets contained similar headpieces at this time. Normally these were removed when fighting, but contemporary illustrations show that some knights preferred wearing them even during battle. (Author's Collection)

tax records. Bernabò would never see freedom again, dying in prison the following December – a bowl of poisoned beans responsible for his untimely demise, according to Milanese historians. One fly had already been caught in the Count of Virtue's parlour, the Visconti spider waiting patiently for other victims in the centre of his expanding web.

A NOT-SO PHONEY WAR

Gian Galeazzo lost no time in asserting his position in northern Italy. In August 1385 he signed an alliance treaty with Francesco da Carrara, Niccolò and Alberto d'Este, lords of Ferrara, and Francesco Gonzaga, lord of Mantua. Ostensibly, the new league was supposed to be directed against marauding mercenary companies but, in reality, despite protestations to the contrary, was in support of the Patriarchy of Aquileia and in opposition to the Venetian-Veronese coalition. Gian Galeazzo had tried to pull Antonio Della Scala into the confederation, a move Venetian diplomacy managed to thwart by playing on the lord of Verona's fear of Carrara's growing power.

Antonio's concerns were not baseless. In July the renowned mercenary captain Giovanni d'Azzo degli Ubaldini had asked for free passage for his troops through Veronese territory, officially to fight the Paduans, with whom, however, he had already struck a secret deal. Della Scala, sensing something not quite right, forbade entrance to Ubaldini, only to encounter a similar refusal from Carrara when he requested his own troops' passage through Padua's lands to

The castle of Marostica played an important role as a safe location for the Veronese during its war with Padua. Frequently the Veronese army stopped there on its movement toward or from Paduan territory. The castle would remain in use until 1587. (Bridgeman Images)

Friuli. Antonio had by now fathomed the extent of the Visconti-Carrara threat and in the end kept his soldiers home, despite Venetian protests. In response to Venice's insistence that he ignore Carrara's ban, in October Della Scala instead moved his forces to the stronghold of Marostica, in order to cover the roads to Treviso, Padua and the Friuli. As a countermove, Carrara positioned his own troops at Bassano del Grappa to block any potential Veronese inroads. Once again rebuffed in his requests for a free passage to the Friuli, in November Antonio sent his army south under the command of his brother-in-law Cortesia da Serego. The Veronese entered Paduan lands by the way of Montagnana, leaving in their wake a trail of destruction before returning into home territory by crossing the Adige River at Castelbaldo.

Carrara's protests following the invasion met but vague responses from Della Scala about possible Venetian responsibilities. As a result, the lord of Padua ordered a retaliatory raid the following December. Paduan forces staged a two-pronged attack on Verona's lands, while pillaging the soldiers touting the Patriarch of Aquileia's name – a mocking tit for tat to Della Scala's shamefaced excuses. War between the two city-states now inevitable, Venice decided to back in full Verona's effort against Padua, on 28 December forming a new league with the object of overthrowing Carrarra. The following February, the Venetians further agreed to fund the war effort on Della Scala's behalf. In the meantime, the Paduans had not remained idle; the same month Carrara also ordered another raid against Verona. The expedition did not enter far into enemy territory but managed to defeat an opposing army, returning to Padua loaded with booty and prisoners.

Wishing to make peace, Urban VI sent Fernando, titular Patriarch of Jerusalem, to sideline Alençon, effectively removing the original source of the conflict. But in any case, the political situation in northern Italy had already reached a point of no return, diplomacy deafened by the sound of clanging weapons.

Meanwhile, in his Milanese parlour, the spider, Count of Virtue, waited patiently.

CHRONOLOGY

1346	Battle of Crécy, English defeat French; Hawkwood may have been present.
1356	Battle of Poitiers, English defeat French; King Jean II captured; Hawkwood may have been present.
1360, 8 May	Treaty of Brétigny brings peace to the Hundred Years War.
1361	Sir John Hawkwood comes to Italy as a member of the 'White Company'.
1363	Hawkwood becomes a captain of the White Company.
1363	Hawkwood under contract to Giovanni II, marquess of Montferrat.
1364–66	Hawkwood leads Pisan army.
1364, 28 July	First Battle of Cascina, Florence defeats Pisa; Hawkwood saves command by tactical retreat.
1368–72	Hawkwood fights for Milan.
1369, December	Second Battle of Cascina (Milan defeats Florence).
1372–77	Hawkwood fights for the Papal States.
1372, 2 June	Battle of Rubiera (Milan defeats Papal States).
1372	War between Padua and Venice (Venice defeats Padua).
1375	Great Raid through Tuscany.
1375	Cansignorio Della Scala, Lord of Verona, dies, leaving illegitimate sons, Bartolomeo and Antonio as governors of the city.
1375–78	War of the Eight Saints (Hawkwood commands Papal States forces to 1377).
1377–80	Hawkwood fights for several Italian states.
1378	Great Western Schism starts with Popes in Rome (Urban VI) and Avignon (Clement VII).
1378–81	Chioggia War (Venice defeats Genoa).
1378–79	Verona repulses an invasion by Milan (Hawkwood and Lutz von Landau leave Milanese service in middle of campaign).
1380–94	Hawkwood under employ of Florence.
1384	Francesco il Vecchio Carrara conquers Treviso.
1385, 6 June	Bernabò Visconti ousted as Duke of Milan by nephew Gian Galeazzo Visconti.

1385, 28 December	League of Venice, Verona and rebel cities of Friuli formed to fight Padua.
1386, 8 March	Veronese army gathers to begin campaign against Padua.
1386, April–June	Verona and Padua fight several small battles, raids, sieges and skirmishes.
1386, 21–23 June	Veronese commander, Cortesia da Serego, surprises Paduans by bringing his army in front of the city walls.
1386, 25 June	Battle of the Brentelle (Padua defeats Verona).
1386, mid-September	Verona appoints Lutz von Landau commander of army.
1386, October	Landau conducts successful operations in Paduan territory.
1386, December	Hawkwood hired by Padua.
1386, end of December	Despite successes, Landau loses Veronese command.
1387, 9 February	Paduan army enters Veronese territory (joined by Hawkwood's force a few days later).
1387, mid-February to 8 March	After conducting a series of successful raids, Paduan army forced to retreat for lack of victuals.
1387, 10 March	Hawkwood and other leaders set up defensive line behind ditch in the proximity of *bastida* of Castagnaro.
1387, 11 March	Battle of Castagnaro (Padua, under Hawkwood's command, defeats Verona).
1387, mid-March	Victorious Paduan army feted by Francesco il Vecchio in Padua.
1387, end April	Hawkwood returns to Florence, his contract expired.
1387, 13 October	Antonio Della Scala flees Verona; dies the same year.
1388, end May	Milan, Venice, Mantua and Ferrara form league against Padua.
1388, 29 June	Francesco il Vecchio abdicates and is replaced by son as lord of Padua.
1389, 11 February	Francesco Novello Carrara cedes Padua and other possessions to Gian Galeazzo Visconti.
1390–92	Florentine War vs. Milan (Milan defeats Florence; Hawkwood retreats saving Florentine army).
1393, 6 November	Francesco il Vecchio Carrara dies in Monza.
1394, March	Sir John Hawkwood dies in Florence.
1406, 17 January	Francesco Novello is strangled to death in a Venetian jail.
1436	Hawkwood's portrait by Paolo Uccello is painted on wall of Florence's Duomo.

OPPOSING COMMANDERS

VERONESE COMMANDERS

Blood may be thicker than water, but in the case of **Antonio Della Scala**, lord of Verona, that haematic fluid had been diluted enough to retain only his forebears' ruthlessness without their political ability. The illegitimate son of Cansignorio Della Scala and his mistress Margherita dei Pittati, Antonio nevertheless received a complete education in everything he might need to govern a city or lead an army. Only 12 when he and his elder brother Bartolomeo became the city's chief executives in 1375, for the following six years Antonio grew impatient under the tutelage of the experienced Guglielmo Bevilacqua and the other members of the regency council appointed by Cansignorio. In 1381 he masterminded his brother's murder in order to become sole ruler of Verona, and the following year married Samaritana da Polenta, daughter of the lord of Ravenna. Samaritana and her relatives soon

The Della Scala (Scaliger) family had been *podestas* (governors) of Verona since the early 13th century. They sought to expand its boundaries on numerous occasions, frequently against Padua. Fighting was incessant between 1328 and 1387, when the loss at Castagnaro chased the last Della Scala *podesta*, Antonio, from the city, never to return. These Della Scala arms are found on the Castel d'Ario. (Roberto Binetti/Alamy Stock Photo)

replaced Bevilacqua and Antonio's other former advisers. As a result, when facing the political crisis caused by the defeat at Castagnaro, Della Scala could count no longer on the backing of Verona's city elite.

Giovanni degli Ordelaffi was fully aware of how crucial the support of the local citizenry could be. When still an infant in 1359, a popular uprising forced his family into exile from his native Forlì that year, although the Ordelaffi managed to return to Forlì as the city's lords in 1379. Not having the finances to raise and support an army, Giovanni became the leader of his own band of *condottieri*: when necessary these could defend Forlì from attack, but if the city was unthreatened he could hire them out to fight others' battles, as at Castagnaro. Physically somewhat of a caricature – more than one source describing him as tall, corpulent, white-skinned, practically beardless and with an ungraceful gait – he nevertheless possessed a sharp mind and political acumen, combined with personal bravery and a total lack of scruples. A solid, if not brilliant military leader, Ordelaffi knew how to wage war for his own and his employers' advantage, and always with an eye to outsmart his relatives in the constant struggle for the lordship of Forlì.

Ruthlessness, treachery and mistrust were key traits of **Ostasio da Polenta**, Antonio Della Scala's brother-in-law. Son of Guido, lord of Ravenna, despite the young age (presumably in his mid-20s) and military inexperience, his blood connection with Verona's ruler had brought him a key position in the Della Scala army – indeed, the prominence given to him in some contemporary chronicles suggests that he, rather than Ordelaffi, was in overall command. Ostasio would show greater skill in political manoeuvres than in military ones, later becoming, albeit briefly, lord of his native city.

Benedetto da Malcesine was another with close links to Antonio Della Scala, having been one of his brother Bartolomeo's murderers in 1381. Benedetto's loyalty would be rewarded with a plum military appointment, as the commander of one of the army's divisions, despite his limited military experience. Equally new in commanding a division was **Taddeo dal Verme**, despite coming from a lineage of soldiers. His family had been readmitted into Verona only a decade before Castagnaro, having spent a quarter of a century in exile for political dissent. Taddeo's first command of troops dated back only to 1386, although in the following years he would earn good military standing under the Visconti banner. The Florentine exile **Giovanni dell'Ischia** (also known as Giovanni dell'Isola) had been in the service of Bernabò Visconti for some years before switching his allegiance to Verona. A brave and daring soldier, Ischia had acquired a reputation as an infantry leader and at Castagnaro would be placed in command of the Veronese foot.

At the battle of Castagnaro, Giovanni degli Ordelaffi led an army of *condottieri* fighting for Verona. He was a good military leader, brave and smart, but he could not prohibit the defeat of his and allies' troops. He would survive the battle only to be poisoned by his son in 1399. These are the family arms from Forli. (The History Collection/ Alamy Stock Photo)

PADUAN COMMANDERS

Francesco 'il Vecchio' (the Elder) da Carrara had been lord of Padua for 37 years at the time of Castagnaro, his rise to power including the arrest and imprisonment of his uncle and co-ruler Giacomino. A shrewd and ambitious

Despite his young age (mid-20s), Ostasio da Polenta, Antonio Della Scala's brother-in-law, may have been in command of the Veronese army on the battlefield of Castagnaro. It was a position earned by familial connection not military capabilities, as seen in the results. The effigy memorializing Ostasio's death in 1396 is from the Basilica of San Francesco in Ravenna. (Author's Collection)

Francesco I 'il Vecchio' da Carrara, the lord of Padua, made his son, Francesco II 'il Novello' da Carrara, titular commander of the Paduan forces at Castagnaro – although both acknowledged John Hawkwood's superior tactical acumen. The younger Carrara acquitted himself well in the battle. In the middle of the bottom of this fresco, from the wall of the Oratorio di San Michele in Padua, painted by Jacopo da Verona in 1397, 'il Novello' wears a black hat. (Photo by Paolo e Federico Manusardi/Electa/Mondadori Portfolio via Getty Images)

politician, Francesco harboured desires to become the paramount leader in northern Italy, leading him to butt heads with most of his neighbours at one stage or another. At the time of the final battle against Verona he was too old to take the field in person, delegating his military duties to his son **Francesco 'il Novello' (the Younger) da Carrara**. A chip off the old block, Carrara junior would often demonstrate his father's ability and determination; however, once too often he let the rash trait of his character rule his decisions, paying little heed to more sober advice, something that in the years to come would lead to his untimely demise at the end of a Venetian noose in 1406.

At the time of Castagnaro, Padua commanded the services of some of the best military leaders of the day. Most famous, the celebrated English captain **Sir John Hawkwood** (Giovanni Acuto to the Italians), the second son of a wealthy landowner from Sible Hedingham, in Essex, who had learned his trade and likely gained his title – if it was earned and not just assumed – during the early stages of the Hundred Years War. Hawkwood possibly fought at Crécy, Poitiers and Brignais. His first sojourn in Italy was in 1361 as a member of the White Company, in service to Giovanni II, marquess of Montferrat, but it is in 1363 that, first as a soldier, and later as captain of the White Company, he gained his renown. From 1368 to 1372 he fought for Milan, from 1372 to 1377 for the Papal States, from 1377 to 1380 for several different cities, and from 1380 until his death in 1394 under contract to Florence, but if not needed by that

city, free to work for anyone he liked. He was not always successful in every engagement in a war, but he earned a reputation for tactical ingenuity, rapacity and for scrupulous adherence to the terms of his military contracts – the last of these, however, not always true. By the time of Castagnaro he had acquired a considerable fortune as well as extensive lands in Tuscany and Umbria, his fame and connections leading him to be chosen by King Richard II of England for various diplomatic missions in Italy. It is therefore understandable that Francesco 'il Vecchio' would be so keen to hire him against Verona, Carrara's money well spent as it turned out.

Also present in the Paduan ranks was Hawkwood's old confederate, **Giovanni d'Azzo degli Ubaldini**. Scion of a warlike family from the Tuscan Apennines, Ubaldini was deemed one of the ablest soldiers of his day and deservedly the victor of the battle of Brentelle in 1386. Although considered by some of his contemporaries to be equal to Hawkwood, Ubaldini thought otherwise and was more than happy to cede command of the Paduan army to Sir John during the Castagnaro campaign, even if – considering the edgy relationship between Hawkwood and Francesco Novello – Giovanni may have wished to pass this 'no win' responsibility to someone else.

The younger Carrara had no clashes, instead, with the leader of the Paduan infantry **Bartolomeo Cermisone da Parma**. Of humble origins, as a young man Cermisone had impressed Francesco il Vecchio with his skill in weapon handling and under his guidance the Carrara foot had developed into a flexible, if by no means large, fighting force. His dedication would pay dividends both at the battle of the Brentelle and again at Castagnaro.

This drawing of Gian Galeazzo Visconti was made by Antonio di Puccio Pisano (better known as Pisanello). Depending on when Pisanello was born (dates range between 1390 and 1395) it could have been made shortly before to up to 20 years after the Milanese duke's death in 1402. It currently hangs in the Louvre Museum in Paris. (Photo by © Alinari Archives/CORBIS/Corbis via Getty Images)

THE HIDDEN LEADERS

The 1385–1387 conflict between Padua and Verona was essentially a war by proxy between Milan and Venice, the open military manoeuvres of the smaller cities mirrored by hidden diplomatic ones of the larger states. The lord of Milan, **Gian Galeazzo Visconti**, would push both contenders while waiting for the right moment to reap for himself the benefits of the struggle.

The **Republic of Venice**, with its multi-voiced political decision-making, had a more expedient goal, to hope that Verona would weaken Padua enough that Francesco il Vecchio would pull out of the war in Friuli. However, like Visconti, Venice would not be averse to opportunistically exploiting the situation's developments to its own advantage.

OPPOSING FORCES

At Castagnaro both armies were remarkably similar in composition and organization, the most significant difference being the English contingent on the Paduan side. However, this apparent uniformity should not blind us to the subtle variations within the opposing forces.

COMPANIES AND *CONDOTTIERI*

The Hundred Years War had been lucrative for many soldiers, especially following the black death, which not only reduced available numbers, but also meant that those still alive could continue to fight and earn higher wages – the demand was the same, while supply was scarcer – as well as any booty they might take. However, if there was no war, there was no pay or plunder; and after the battle of Poitiers in 1356 and the Treaty of Brétigny in 1360, warfare in France was cut back significantly, especially by the English. Unemployed soldiers immediately became a problem. Some returned to their homes, although normal labour proved neither as lucrative nor adventurous as their previous employment. A few turned to outlawry, while others became protectors against outlaws.

But most stayed in the military profession, offering their services to anyone who would pay them, usually joining with others as companies of mercenaries. Flemings, Hainauters, Germans, Spanish and French all joined, but most new mercenaries seem to have been English or Gascons. Nobility did not preclude mercenary employment, but many, including leaders, were non-nobles. One of the earliest leaders was Arnaud de Cervole, a defrocked priest, possibly a chaplain, who was known by the title 'archpriest'.

Cervole was one of the founders of the 'Great Company' in 1357. This mercenary army grew quickly to 2,000, large enough to cause significant damage to the lands they pillaged. With the king of France captured by the English at Poitiers, the Great Company knew that raiding lands in France would not be very profitable, so they raided the lands around Avignon, residence of the pope, Innocent VI. In 1357–58 they ravaged Provence and sacked Sainte-Maximin, prompting a payment of 20,000 florins from the Pope for the mercenaries to disband and leave the region. Two years later,

chieza oltra il debito dadio ordinato : Come meſſ Johanni aguto cha ualco inful terreno e contado difirenza :

the Great Company re-formed and raided the Rhone Valley and Languedoc. Finally, in 1362 a French army decided to put an end to these activities and met and defeated the Great Company in battle, at Brignais, but the mercenaries continued to pillage Languedoc and Auvergne. This brought another 40,000 florins from the Pope, as well as his absolution for what they had done.

However, plunder of France could sustain a large number of mercenaries for only so long. The War of the Two Pedros fought in Spain between 1356 and 1375 drew some away. But even more profitable was Italy and its many

In this illumination from Giovanni Sercambi's *Le croniche di Lucca*, John Hawkwood and his mercenaries are shown riding outside of Florence. It is difficult to know which of these soldiers is Hawkwood, but his name, in the text above (Johanni aguto) is easily read. (Archivio di Stato di Lucca, Ms 107, f. 98r. Authorization 87/19. Su concessione del Ministero dei Beni e delle Attività Culturali e del Turismo. Duplicazione e riproduzione vietata con qualsiasi mezzo)

This late 14th-century Northern Italian manuscript of Guiron le Courtois depicts three Arthurian knights. Two wear the great helm, while the third wears a bascinet, its visor raised, but with his mail aventail still tied around the bottom half of his face. Their lances are carried by their squires. (Bibliotheque nationale de France, Département des manuscrits, NAF 5243)

wars. Plus, the cities involved in them were wealthy and willing to pay for others to fight for them. Mercenary bands had been active in Italy since the end of the 13th century, initially Catalan and then French and German, a fallout of the constant foreign interference in Italian affairs. The English would arrive only after the Treaty of Brétigny, bringing with them the tactical innovations developed in the first stages of the Hundred Years War. It did not take long for Italians to follow suit, first as part of foreign mercenary bands and then creating their own companies. By the 1380s the Italian element predominated in the various armies milling round Italy, establishing a long-standing contractual military system known as the *condotta militare* (roughly: *military contract*), or simply *condotta*, the recipient of such legal agreement called a *condottiere*.

Condotte were elaborate documents, becoming more standardized over time. Company leaders would strike similar agreements with the individual *condottieri* of their band. *Condotte* specified the terms and length of employment, plus matters such as the number of soldiers or units, horse and foot, individual pay and equipment, billets, adding, sometimes, other provisions such as the replacement of horses lost in action. Companies were usually hired for short spans, even for as little as four months, usually coinciding with the campaign season. This, however, led to the unwelcome phenomenon of marauding unemployed mercenary bands; for instance, after his contract with pope Urban VI expired in June 1383, John Hawkwood and Giovanni degli Ubaldini formed a 'free company' of a few thousand men that proceeded to extort money from a number of cities from Naples to Lucca, pillaging the countryside as they went.

For this reason, and to have at their disposal on a permanent basis the best military talents on the market, by the end of the 14th century some of the most far-sighted of Italy's rulers had started to offer longer-term contracts, also trying to tie top-notch *condottieri* to their state or person by granting them land and fiefs or through blood ties – Bernabò Visconti had two of his daughters married to famous mercenary captains. In the meantime, some Italian rulers, like the Gonzaga of Mantua or the Malatesta of Rimini, were in turn becoming military entrepreneurs, with the twofold objective of preserving their own possessions (frequently against rival claimants) and getting someone else to foot the bill of their army's upkeep. During the Paduan–Veronese war of 1385–87, Ostasio da Polenta, son of the lord of Ravenna, would bring his own company to serve under his brother-in-law Antonio Della Scala.

Mounted troops were the mainstay of a 14th-century mercenary unit; yet, despite recent scholarly investigation, a lot

The soldier witnessing the martyrdom of St Bartholomew is dressed in typical infantry armour from mid-14th-century Northern Italy: plate leg and knee armour, shield, mail coif and kettle-hat. It was painted by Pacino di Bonaguida, *c.*1340, in Florence and now resides in the Metropolitan Museum of Art, Cloisters Collection. (The Metropolitan Museum of Art, New York)

of unanswered questions remain about their make-up. By the 1380s most contracts outline payment for a specific number of *lance* – lances; what this meant for operations is open to opinion. Although in the early 1360s the three-man cavalry lance was indeed a tactical subdivision within an army, a quarter of a century later it was very likely becoming an administrative convention. Originally devised as a combat trio of two men-at-arms with one assistant, the lance was ideally suited for fighting on foot, a trend in Italian warfare even before being made popular by veterans of the Hundred Years War. However, the last two decades of the century witnessed a revival of cavalry in battle, innovative tactics combined with technologically advanced armour leading to the optimization of horse units. It did not take long for the 20–25-man mounted squadron, rather than the lance, to become the core of Italian mercenary companies.

THE POLITICAL-MILITARY SETTING

By the middle of the 14th century, Italian city-states enjoyed substantial material wealth but militarily were almost bankrupt. Only fragments of the old Communal militias remained active, economic issues arguing against diverting substantial sections of a city's workforce for war. Therefore, in the long run it was cheaper and socio-economically less disruptive to entrust someone else with the fighting, costly as it may have been in the short term. Bigger states had similar problems. The papacy's absence from Italy for 70 years – from 1305 to 1376, the pontiff's residence moving to Avignon in 1309 – meant an increased fraying of the relationship between the popes and their main military force, the local lords, their loyalty at best fickle. Baronial unrest also plagued the kingdom of Naples. The Italian situation in its entirety favoured the rise of the mercenary, warfare being one of the few ways allowing the many Italian petty, or important, lords to live and survive. The constant state of conflict between the various states meant also a steady demand for professional fighters, even better if they came as organized forces.

THE FORCES

The overlapping of the administrative with the tactical creates endless headaches for those investigating late medieval Italian warfare, Castagnaro being a case in point. Our main source for the battle is the so-called *Cronaca Carrarese* by Galeazzo Gatari; and the same work as rewritten by his son, Andrea. When talking about the two armies, the older and younger Gatari give wildly different numbers. To complicate matters further, Galeazzo specifies that Hawkwood's contingent included 500 men-at-arms (*uomini d'arme*), yet refers

This very rare early suit of armour from Churburg Castle (dating to the time of Castagnaro) contains plate gauntlets (covering the hands and wrists), vambraces (lower arms), couters (elbows) and cuirass (torso). A visored bascinet and aventail protected the head and neck. Inscriptions and design show that these were all made by the same armourer and meant to be worn together. Unfortunately, the mail shirt, leg armour and gauntlet extensions have not survived. (Photo by Sergio Anelli/Electa/Mondadori Portfolio via Getty Images)

Although painted more than 40 years after John Hawkwood's death, Paolo Uccello's equestrian fresco shows an accurate likeness of the mercenary leader. In 1387, fighting for Padua, Hawkwood played a decisive role in the battle of Castagnaro against the Veronese. (Photo by © Alinari Archives/CORBIS/Corbis via Getty Images)

to all other mounted troops as 'horses' (*cavalli*), only to revert to men-at-arms when talking about prisoners.

We are also left with the question of if and how the *saccomanni*, light cavalrymen entrusted with foraging and raiding, were counted. These existed more by default than by design, not every man-at-arms having the money to buy a full suit of armour. Thus one can speculate that the *saccomanni* formed the rear ranks of a battle array, although one contemporary chronicle, by Piero Minerbetti – admittedly not very reliable – has the Paduan ones at Castagnaro acting akin to a vanguard or a forlorn hope.

At Castagnaro, about a quarter of the two armies' combat element was made up of non-Italians. Out of 80 known Veronese senior and junior cavalry leaders (*caporali*), 18 were German, quite natural considering that until a few weeks before Verona's commander-in-chief had been Lutz von Landau. The elusive Count d'Ancre (whom Andrea Gatari calls the 'Count d'Erre'), commanding one of Della Scala's divisions and tentatively identified with the seasoned *condottiere* Ulrich Trottinger, may also be German. Some Germans were also present within the Paduan ranks, but for sure Carrara's most important foreign element was John Hawkwood's English company of 500 men-at-arms and as many archers, providing the Paduans with a crucial tactical edge.

Italian employers found English longbowmen difficult to place in a precise administrative bracket, given that they rode into battle and fought dismounted. This put them somewhere in the middle, between cavalry and infantry, as in Galeazzo Gatari's chronicle. Whatever the bureaucratic or popular perception, at the time of Castagnaro, English archers had been a constant, albeit limited, feature of Italian warfare for nearly 30 years, commanding high enlistment prices. As we shall see below, the English

By the middle of the 14th century, metal plates protecting the vulnerable knees and lower legs of cavalry had supplemented mail leggings. Initially covering only the front of the leg, they were strapped on top of mail armour, although by this time both the poleyns (knee) and greaves (calves) would surround the entire leg, replacing the mail entirely. (The Metropolitan Museum of Art, New York)

tactical set-up at Castagnaro allowed Hawkwood to maximize his army's potential by getting the bowmen to work closely with the men-at-arms.

It is often repeated that late Communal Italian infantry was solely trained for defence, the pavisiers, spearmen and crossbowmen little more than a static formation. In reality, contemporary sources often show crossbowmen acting as skirmishers ahead of the front line, in combination with the highly flexible sword-and-buckler soldiers, also armed with an array of staff weapons. Besides, Communal militias had in many cases been integrated in the seigniorial system, creating a category of semi-professional soldiers. At the end of the 14th century, Francesco Gonzaga of Mantua made a census of all the men in his domain outside of Mantua suitable for military service, 2,436 in total. An indefinite number of these joined the ranks of his *provvisionati*, semi-professional infantrymen paid a regular stipend or *provvisione*. The Visconti of Milan had a long-standing policy of employing troops drawn from their territories to serve as the lords' bodyguard.

Both Padua and Verona had their own groups of *provvisionati*; however, the Paduan infantry could count on the leadership of Bartolomeo Cermisone, who had commanded it since the Chioggia War, thus providing uniformity in training and tactical outlook. The Veronese foot was not so lucky, its commander Giovanni dell'Ischia relatively new to the job. As a result, at Castagnaro the Veronese infantry put up a stiff fight, but little more than that. In addition, the rabble (*canaglia*) that had swollen the Veronese ranks would prove more of a hindrance than a help.

The field in which the Veronese clearly had the edge was field artillery: 12 carts with multi-barrelled gunpowder pieces. Galeazzo Gatari was sufficiently impressed (and concerned) to give a detailed description of these contraptions. It would be up to Hawkwood and other Paduan commanders to deny this technological advantage to their enemies.

ARMS AND ARMOUR

Paolo Uccello's portrait of Sir John Hawkwood on the side of the Duomo in Florence is justifiably famous. Uccello was already a painter of renown when, in 1436, he took on the commission of an equestrian fresco of the

RIGHT

The bascinet appeared as early as the mid-13th century and until *c*.1450 was the most popular style of helmet used by all soldiers everywhere in Europe. This was undoubtedly because it could be fitted with a visor of various shapes hinged either at the top or along the side or worn open. This example is from the Metropolitan Museum of Art's collection and is dated to the Castagnaro period. (The Metropolitan Museum of Art, New York)

FAR RIGHT

A visor could be hinged at the sides of the bascinet, such as this one from the Metropolitan Museum of Art, but could also be attached at the centre of the top. As artworks from the period show, by 1380 bascinets fitted with visors had become very popular. While frequently referred to as 'pig-faced' bascinets, the term 'visored bascinet' was more common at the time. (The Metropolitan Museum of Art, New York)

OPPOSITE

Although plates of steel were increasingly covering the late 14th-century soldier's body, the mail shirt was still in use, either alone or supplemented by plates placed over and sometimes attached to the mail – depending on their availability and the soldier's wealth. With the mail aventail also worn, as in this example from the Royal Armouries, soldiers were well protected from all but the most intense blows to their torso, shoulders, neck or upper arms. (Royal Armouries)

famous English mercenary, who had died in Florence two generations before. Uccello, born three years after Hawkwood's death in 1394, had never seen the man. But, as the city's Signoria had voted to memorialize the condottieri leader from before his death, previous portraits existed and, it is speculated, that these, principally that made by Agnolo Gaddi in 1396, served as inspiration for Uccello to reproduce an image that could be recognizable to any who had met Hawkwood.

Uccello might have accurately painted facial features, height, maybe even the size and shape of his hands. (It is speculated that the mortuary mask of Hawkwood existed.) But what of what he wears? Hawkwood appears completely encased in a suit of steel plate armour, the pieces all made to fit and work together. But Uccello was portraying the armour of the 1430s, and not of the 1390s that Hawkwood would have worn. Much had changed between those two periods. The armour made then would still have covered the whole body and been of the finest quality, but it would not have been as integrated as an entire suit of plate from three decades later. As can be seen in several art works, late 14th-century armour could also have had mail attached to protect vulnerable parts of the body, the neck, the groin and the armpits.

Hawkwood's helmet is not depicted in the Uccello work, his head bearing a cap sometimes called a 'captain's cap' as it is depicted on other *condottieri*, a symbol of leadership. Of course, when Hawkwood was on the battlefield, he wore a helmet. From about 1300 to about 1420 in Italy the most common cavalry helmet, worn by both knights and men-at-arms, was the bascinet. Most early bascinets had a conical shape, close fitting to the sides and rear of the head, and sometimes descending to the base of the neck and cheeks; however, by the middle of the 14th century, shorter bascinets with mail aventails attached to the helmet to cover the neck and shoulders, were becoming more common. And by the time of the battle of Castagnaro, almost all were fitted with a visor. The visor was rounded and hinged at the left side of the helmet at first, although in the majority of illustrations where the visor can be seen in the late 14th century, the hinge was attached to the

FAR LEFT
From about 1330 mail aventails were frequently attached to bascinets. These would completely cover the neck, shoulders, and when drawn up and tied, as this from the Metropolitan Museum of Art is, the face as well. (When not in combat, the aventail descended down the front of the armour like a bib.) Aventails were attached to the helmet by iron pegs known as vervelles. (The Metropolitan Museum of Art, New York)

LEFT
This suit of armour, found in the Churburg Castle collection, dates from around 20 years after Castagnaro. It does, however, present an integrated armour like those worn by many knights and men-at-arms on the battlefield. It combines steel plate on the legs, knees, upper arms, elbows and torso with a mail shirt and visored bascinet. (DeAgostini/ Getty Images)

centre of the top of the face opening. The so-called 'pig-faced bascinet', where the visor has a pointed, rather than a round shape, became common throughout Europe by 1380. Contemporary art works show Italian infantry also favoured bascinets, although more frequently wearing them without visors than the cavalry. Popular elsewhere in Europe, kettle-hats seem not to have been as common in Italy by the time of Castagnaro, although the simple steel cap can be seen in illustrations, undoubtedly worn by those who could not afford or acquire a bascinet.

New carburizing processes and the use of the blast furnace during the 14th century allowed steel to become the principal metal for armour and helmet construction. The greater protection of plate armour would mean over the years the abandonment of the layers of mail and cloth padding, an arming doublet with mail reinforcements in exposed points the only undergarment necessary. Not only did this increase the defensive capabilities of the plates from which armour and helmets were constructed, but steel could also be polished to a high shine. One of the reasons the White Company was called such, alleges Florentine chronicler Filippo Villani, is that they polished their armour 'so shiny that when they appear in combat their armour looked like mirrors, and thus they were even more frightening'.

Still, at the time of Castagnaro, it was only the wealthiest of soldiers who could afford these state-of-the-art armours. Sir John Hawkwood could have done so, as could many of his well-paid *condottieri*. However, most cavalry soldiers would have worn a mixture of plate and mail armour, some passed down, acquired from the battlefield or bought used, as well as some new pieces. This was true even in the 15th century, with various inventories of Florentine armour merchants between 1424 and 1427 showing a wide array of ages and styles of their wares. Old helmets with mail aventails could be bought at a far inferior price than newer helmets, priced at seven florins – two months'

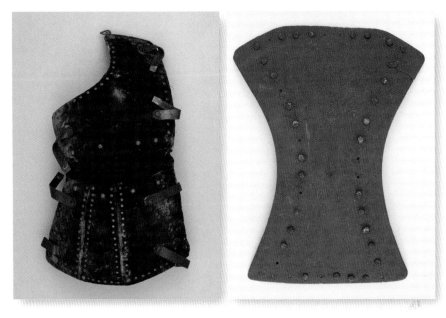

wages for a skilled worker at the time; a new pair of Florentine cuisses was worth five florins, as much as a pair of Milanese refurbished ones.

The expense of plate armour generally excluded its use by infantry soldiers, although by the end of the 14th century a few of the more wealthy foot-soldiers began to adopt its use, especially to cover the breast, back and limbs. Others, especially urban militias and less wealthy mercenaries, wore mail shirts and helmets, sometimes with the addition of a breastplate and plates covering the limbs. For the very poorest, armour might be nothing more than a quilted jacket or leather jerkin.

Cloth-covered armours increased in use by infantry and cavalry during the 14th century. Chief among these in Italy was the brigandine, made from small rectangular plates of iron, overlapping each other, and riveted to a fabric coat fastened up the front or on one side. The iron plates of brigandines, very prone to rust, especially from the sweat produced in the extremes of battle,

were coated with a layer of lead and tin. Worn alone or over a padded felt or leather undergarment, brigandines were quite protective, able to turn a swung sword or staff weapon. Worn over other armour, mail or plate, they protected wearers even against the strongest of sharp-edged weapon thrusts and blunt-force weapon blows. So effective was this armour that luxurious brigandines, made of expensive silks and brocades, were worn away from the battlefield for protection against attack and assassination.

Given the high costs of late medieval armour, but also its necessity, many soldiers resorted to leasing their weapons. A shrewd businessman like the merchant of Prato, Francesco Datini (1335–1410), made a handsome profit by leasing out military equipment during the campaign season; what was still serviceable at the end of the above was refurbished and awaited the next season. Datini was particularly active in the arms trade, any peace treaty a chance to buy up surplus equipment at a reduced price, ready to be sold at its full worth once hostilities resumed.

As plate armours became more prevalent, the use of shields began to decline. For cavalry the flat or slightly curved, medium-sized triangular shield remained most popular, although oblong, round and even leaf-shaped shields are reported. Triangular shields were less used by the infantry, who preferred the targe (a small shield affixed to the left forearm and hand), buckler (a small round shield held by the hand) or pavise (a very large oblong or rectangular shield that could be propped up by a wooden brace or held in two hands by a separate 'pavisier', generally to protect spearmen, archers, crossbowmen and, in the 15th century, handgunners). Most shields were wood covered in leather or thin metal plate.

Arms and armour historians have long disputed whether improvements in armour led to improvements in arms or vice versa. At no time in history is this more difficult to determine than the last two centuries of the Middle Ages.

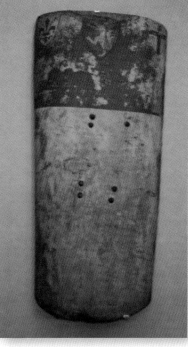

FAR LEFT
Two soldiers observe the beheading of St James in a detail from the altar of St James in the Cathedral of St Zeno in Pistoia, carved by Leonardo di Ser Giovanni in 1361–71. Neither is wealthy. The soldier in front wears an open-faced bascinet attached to a mail aventail and a mail shirt. Plates over the shoulders and elbows are leather or cuir-bouilli rather than metal. He carries a buckler. The soldier behind him differs in wearing a kettle-hat helmet and carrying a sword which is similar to that wielded by the executioner. (DeAgostini/ Getty Images)

LEFT
This long and wide shield, an Italian invention from at least as early as the 13th century – reputably from Pavia, hence its name – was of limited use on the battlefield, as it was simply too large for hand-to-hand combat. However, it did protect crossbowmen who would duck behind it to reload. This pavise is in the Bardini Museum, Florence. (Author's Collection)

The great helm had served knights of every European army well since around 1200, but by the time of the battle of Castagnaro they were beginning to fall out of fashion. Bascinets with visors that could be opened allowed for better breathing and communication than the great helm while not significantly lowering the protection provided by these strong solid helmets. (Royal Armouries)

Longbow archers were known only by reputation in Italy before they began to arrive as mercenaries after 1360. The English mercenary captain, John Hawkwood, would make good use of his longbowmen at the battle of Castagnaro, placing them on an escarpment to shoot into the Veronese left flank. John Gower's archer in *Vox clamantis* shoots a typical longbow of the late 14th century, extra arrows crammed into his belt for easy removal. (Photo by DeAgostini/ Getty Images)

Changes in armour from coats of mail topped by great helms in 1250 to integrated suits of plate armour in 1450 defines innovation and progression at a pace not previously witnessed since the beginning of the Iron Age (if even then). The power and destructive capabilities of gunpowder weapons are used as a rationale by some historians, but gunpowder artillery and handguns do not impact the battlefield until after full plate armours appear in large numbers.

The longbow and crossbow are also credited with motivating change in armour construction. While it is certainly true that the English had used the longbow effectively in numerous engagements against the Scots and French by the end of the 14th century, outside of those enemies few knew of the weapons' power. Because of the difficulty in training skilled longbowmen, with archers needing to learn and practise from childhood onwards, no one else had adopted the weapon; even England worried about sustaining their numbers, with Edward III's 1363 proscription against any other sports being played by English youth as the first of many such laws. English mercenary captains always recruited a force of longbowmen, but never very many – Hawkwood had but 500 at Castagnaro – their small numbers further indicating that this weapon alone could not have influenced the development of plate armours.

Use of the crossbow was more universal throughout Europe, and changes in its construction during the later Middle Ages certainly allowed it to deliver a much more powerful ballistic blow. During the 14th century the standard crossbow, a composite of wood, hide, sinew and glue, was replaced by an entirely wooden crossbow, which increased its power, although not its flexibility. Loading was still primarily done using belt-hooks and stirrups, but cranequins using levers and ratchets to withdraw the bowstring were beginning to replace these. Training a crossbowman, unlike a longbowman, was relatively easy and quick, learning to load the crossbow really the only requirement. Many crossbowmen used in 14th-century Italian battles, including Castagnaro, came from urban militias, these soldiers a constant feature of a city's political make-up. For example, in 1378 Florence raised a force of 1,000 crossbowmen among its citizens, ostensibly for the preservation of law and order.

The rest of the weapons wielded at Castagnaro had appeared on the battlefield for centuries, if not millennia. These included blunt-force weapons: maces, hammers and axes (although the latter were also sharp-edged), and sharp-edged weapons: daggers, spears, lances, staff weapons and swords (the last frequently called *estocs* or *stocchi*).

Blunt-forced weapons were meant to deliver a heavy blow to stun, wound or kill. All were heavy handles topped by bulbous metal heads (maces), square or bulbous heads with a point sticking out of one end, often pointed slightly downward (hammers) or square heads with a blade protruding from one or two ends (axes). The swing was short and powerful, with the blow bruising and bone-breaking. If powerful enough the blow might cause the point or blade to penetrate the steel armour, causing further damage to the body underneath. When aimed at an opponent's head, a concussion or broken skull could result.

By the 1370s the *estoc* had become the most common type of sword in Italy, a weapon that could be swung or thrust – a good swordsman tried to aim at the joints or where plate armour was thinner, such as the sides of a breastplate. A shorter-hilted sword was wielded from horseback, while the infantry used a same-sized or longer-hilted sword (the so-called 'hand-and-a-half sword', as it could be wielded with one or two hands).

Staff-weapons, in their simplest form, were a combination of a spear or lance with an axe, blade, point and/or hammer. A wide range of staff-weapons had developed by 1300, but it was between then and the 17th century that they became an infantry weapon used extensively throughout Europe. There were many types and variants, but wielded primarily by soldiers to slash, thrust, hammer, punch and grab, whatever was needed to disable an opponent.

Ironically, it was the smallest of the sharp-edged weapons, the dagger, that was the most effective against plate-armoured foes. Everyone of every rank, cavalry as well as infantry, carried a dagger. By the time of Castagnaro, soldiers were using many different types. Once an opponent was disabled or stunned, a dagger could easily find a gap in the armour to wound or kill.

There were gunpowder weapons at Castagnaro. The Paduan chronicler Galeazzo Gatari saw these after they had been captured and brought as prizes into Padua, and he leaves a detailed and thorough description. However, the detail of his description also indicates how unusual these guns were: not the guns themselves, which he calls *bonbardelle* (small bombards), nor what they fire, 'stone balls the size of a chicken's egg'. Gunpowder weapons

The sword remained the principle weapon of knights and men-at-arms. The most popular at the time of Castagnaro was the so-called hand-and-a-half sword. Light enough to be wielded with a single hand, it had a hilt long enough to be grasped by two hands. (The Metropolitan Museum of Art, New York)

had been in Europe for more than a half-century by the time of Castagnaro, and while it might be difficult to determine much from the name itself – most gunpowder artillery pieces in Italy at the time were known as *bombarde* – as later bombards and bombardelles would be very large guns, that the calibre was sufficient only to fire egg-sized stone balls, suggests that these were fairly small weapons. They also appear to be muzzle-loaders without removable chambers, as the latter are almost always mentioned in contemporary Italian sources if they were used.

What Gatari seems to find unusual, and therefore in need of clearer, more detailed description, is how the guns were mounted, loaded, fired and transported: 'Then [Della Scala] had made three carts, each equipped with three shelves, one on top of the other. Each of these shelves was divided into four, each quarter carrying twelve small bombards very closely packed together... thus every shelf carried 48 *bombardelles*, for a total of 144 weapons per cart.' In total there were '432 guns',

Staff weapons had been used by infantry in Italy for centuries before the battle of Castagnaro. In this depiction, accompanying a 14th-century copy of Caesar's *De bello civili* (*The Civil War*), painted in Northern Italy (Biblioteca Trivulziana, Milan, MS 691, f. 87r), a soldier's sharp, long-bladed glaive is easily seen, as is the way it is attached to the staff and its metal end-point. (Akg-images/Andre Held)

Every medieval soldier carried a long thin dagger. On the battlefield it often delivered the coup de grace, piercing the neck, armpit or groin underneath the mail armour. This suitably called ballock dagger was one of many styles a soldier could choose from at the end of the 14th century. (The Metropolitan Museum of Art, New York)

he writes later. It is perhaps easy to imagine 12 small guns mounted next to each other on a shelf. Smaller guns were frequently mounted together at this time and would continue to be for the next two centuries at least. Leonardo Da Vinci has illustrations showing this type of mounting among his engineering drawings.

How these shelves were mounted on the cart is not indicated until after Gatari describes the loading and firing procedure:

> On each cart stood three men: one to shoot twelve guns, firing them all in one single volley; then using a mechanical device he would turn the shelf horizontally, pointing the fired guns towards his companions and then repeat the process with the other sides. Once he'd finished firing all four sides of the first shelf he would climb up to the second and his companions below reloaded the fired guns; and so he then proceeded up to the third shelf.

This is less easily understood. One man designated to fire the guns, and two to load them is okay, even that the guns on each shelf are fired in volley. But that there appear to be four shelves on one level and three different levels, and that the man responsible for firing the guns has to climb up to these levels while his assistants reload the discharged guns is rather confusing. Are the shelves mounted on a square tower or a column? Does the firer climb up the outside or the inside? Presumably his assistants also have to climb up to reload the guns on the upper two levels, but how do they do so? What was the 'mechanical device' used to turn the tower? Cranks and levers were known at the time, so the 'mechanical device' was clearly something different, but what it might be otherwise cannot be determined. There are no art works depicting these or similar guns to clarify what Gatari means in his also unique description.

As for transporting the guns, the Paduan chronicler is clearer and more easily understood:

> And each cart was pulled by four tall and big warhorses, covered with *cuir bouilli* over which they carried caparisons of steel. Each of the four horses was ridden by a fully armoured gentleman squire, who with one hand held the bridle and the other a small axe for defence. And when the enemy was fully arrayed, these had to get close to them and have the guns fired, 48 at once, in order to break the Carrara formation and capture their banners.

These were obviously heavy carts. Even with the smallest guns, 144 of them would be heavy, let alone adding the weight of the shelves, tower and mechanical device. Besides, they were pulled by 'four tall, big horses'. These horses were surely strong, having to pull such a heavy cart and further weighed down by cuir bouilli and steel caparisons. Why they wore such protection is explained by the short range of the guns, needing 'to get close to [the enemy]' to disrupt their lines effectively. The horses would have been easily hit targets, with their riders, and presumably the leaders of these gun crews, squires of the 'gentlemen' class, also tasked with protecting the beasts with their small axes.

The Veronese guns were uniquely mounted, and they must have been expensive, with the wages of their crew high, both because of the skill needed for their job as well as the danger of having to load and fire that many early guns. They were also unused at Castagnaro, their capture by the Paduans precluding any shot. Perhaps this is why they do not appear in any artistic or written sources again.

As there are no extant gunpowder weapons securely dated to the 14th century, we cannot determine what those on the multi-gun Veronese engines at Castagnaro looked like. As Galeazzo Gatari describes 144 of them mounted on each engine, 432 total, they cannot have been even as large as this small early gun from the Bardini Museum in Florence. (Author's Collection)

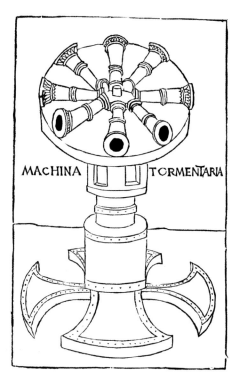

There are no contemporary illustrations that come close to depicting the Veronese gunpowder weapon machines described by Galeazzo Gatari as having been captured at Castagnaro. This rotating wheeled 'machina tormentaria' drawn by Roberto Valturio for his *De Re Militari* of 1475 (but likely never constructed) has only eight guns on this single shelf. (Photo 12/UIG via Getty Images)

OPPOSING PLANS

Around 1370 Altichiero da Zevio painted the Adoration of the Virgin in the Cavalli family chapel in the Church of Sant'Anastasia in Verona. These, Cavalli knights – some of whom would fight at Castagnaro – dressed in armour and bascinets, kneel before the Madonna. The knight in the centre wears a clearly visible hand-and-a-half sword. (The Picture Art Collection/Alamy Stock Photo)

Strictly speaking, no fully shaped plan existed on either side, the clash at Castagnaro arising from a series of circumstances and reactions to them. The Paduans had been forced to retreat for lack of victuals after staging a raid in depth into Veronese territory; at this point a battle was out of the question, given the customary practice of war, which dictated that field encounters be avoided unless absolutely necessary. However, with the looming prospect of his army returning into Paduan territory only to disintegrate in all directions for want of provisions, Francesco Novello da Carrara decided to fight it out. Besides, with a large Veronese force following them and poised to cross the Adige River to wreak havoc on Paduan lands, it made military, as well

as political sense to attempt a stand while still in enemy territory. Besides, should things really deteriorate, there was still the possibility of retreating across the river to the stronghold of Castelbaldo.

Although the presence of multi-barrelled gunpowder artillery with the Veronese forces has been interpreted as evidence of the willingness of that army to seek battle, this comes with the benefit of hindsight and reliance on an author like Andrea Gatari who, writing two generations later, was interested in exalting Padua's past glories. In reality, the Veronese had even less interest in picking a fight than the Paduans, hoping for the greater convenience of starving their opponents into surrender. Or alternatively, by following them into their own territory, they would put pressure on the Carrara regime and, with luck, cause a political revolution in Padua. As such, the multi-barrelled artillery can be seen rather as a deterrent to convince the Paduans *not* to give battle. One of Hawkwood's major achievements in the battle would be neutralizing the Veronese guns.

In this detail of another illustration from the very important *La croniche di Lucca* of Giovanni Sercambi, infantry march from a victorious raid leading prisoners and farm animals. In the background houses and barns burn. For non-combatant peasants war was always a tragedy, their lives and livelihoods often sacrificed without mercy. (Archivio di Stato di Lucca, Ms 107, f. 164v. Authorization 87/19. Su concessione del Ministero dei Beni e delle Attività Culturali e del Turismo. Duplicazione e riproduzione vietata con qualsiasi mezzo)

In this depiction, from the late 14th-century *Queste de Saint Graal*, one of Arthur's knights on his search for the Holy Grail has stopped to bathe in a lake. His armour lies around him, including long-sleeved mail shirt, steel breastplate and shoulder armour, and visored bascinet. The inside of one of his steel couters (elbow armour) is also seen. His sword is sheathed but close enough at hand to be available should he need it. (Bibliothèque nationale de France. Département des manuscrits. Français 343)

THE CAMPAIGN

COURTESY REBUFFED

Hostilities resumed even before the end of winter 1386. Protected by a strong covering force under Cortesia da Serego, in February the Veronese diverted the river Bacchiglione, the main power source of Padua's grain mills. The same strategy had been used 60 years before by Cangrande Della Scala to subdue the same rival city, but this time Francesco il Vecchio managed to contain the damage by diverting other bodies of water into the Bacchiglione's bed. 'Thus he found a way to grind', comments Galeazzo Gatari, 'however, countless misery was inflicted on the people living in both territories'.

Venetian gold had given Della Scala a massive boost in building his forces, his army's strength, known to us thanks to a contemporary administrative document, which also gives us some interesting insights into the needs of a 14th-century expeditionary force.

Array of the army of the magnificent and powerful lord sir Antonio Della Scala against the lord of Padua, this force moving on the 8th day of March 1386

Wagons of bread	1,000
Wagons of wine	800
Wagons with other victuals	400
Wagons of sorghum and spelt	500
Wagons of arrows and bolts	300
Wagons of bombards and artillery, with all their apparatus and munitions	500
Wagons of tents and shacks	50
Wagons of bridges, ladders, bellows, shovels, levers, sawhorses and other instruments	300
Wagons of balls for lanterns	200
Wagons of crossbows and pavises	50
Wagons of rushes and fascines	1,000
Carts of the aforementioned lord, courtiers and citizens	300
Wagons and apparels for all trades	50
Field fortifications (*bastie*) with all their necessities	4
Lances (*lanze*) of mounted soldiers, reviewed and paid for the whole month of March	2,500

Mounted crossbowmen	600
Foot crossbowmen	900
Infantry with 'bolt-proof armour'	1,200
Armoured horsemen with lances	300
Mounted pillagers (*sacardi*)	500
Infantry banners, with 25 [men] per banner	100
Trumpeters	46
Infantry of the Veronese county	5,400
Infantry from the Vicenza area	3,500
Sappers and miners	5,000

Note: The list continues with the gifts prepared by Antonio Della Scala to distribute to his victorious army, including 50 complete suits of armour, silverware, precious cloth, choice foreign wines and 150 ounces (220 imperial ounces) of pearls 'of various sizes'.

The above list, however, is not as clear-cut as it may appear. For instance, the 2,500 presumably Veronese citizens of the infantry banners, appear too high a number for a city with an estimated population of about 15,000 at the beginning of the 15th century. Still, one may hypothesize a demographic drop owing to the city's vicissitudes after 1387, besides the fact that by this date paying for a substitute to take the field was an established practice among members of Italian militias. Whatever the case, the list is a testimony to Antonio Della Scala's massive effort in delivering a decisive and crushing blow against Padua and the Carrara.

Antonio was biding his time, in the meantime milking the Venetians for all their worth. Venice was pressuring the Veronese for a decisive attack against Padua, the Republic on the Lagoon having become ever more frantic after Francesco il Vecchio managed in March to buy from the Archduke of Austria the towns of Feltre and Cividale for 60,000 ducats, thus tightening his grip on the Friuli. Della Scala obliged, at the beginning of April sending the part of his army recruited in Venetian territory – 300 lances, 400 crossbowmen and 400 other infantry – to the outskirts of Treviso. The Veronese army lingered there for a few days before moving towards Sacile,

Two cavalry forces face off before beginning a battle in this illumination from Sercambi's *Le croniche di Lucca*. Dressed the same – plate armour on the legs, arms and hands with mail girdles, but not torso armour apparent under their tunics, heads covered by bascinets and mail aventails – and all carrying lances, the soldiers listen to commands given by trumpeters blowing on their buisines. (Archivio di Stato di Lucca Ms 107, f. 102r. Authorization 87/19. Su concessione del Ministero dei Beni e delle Attività Culturali e del Turismo. Duplicazione e riproduzione vietata con qualsiasi mezzo)

The Brentelle Campaign

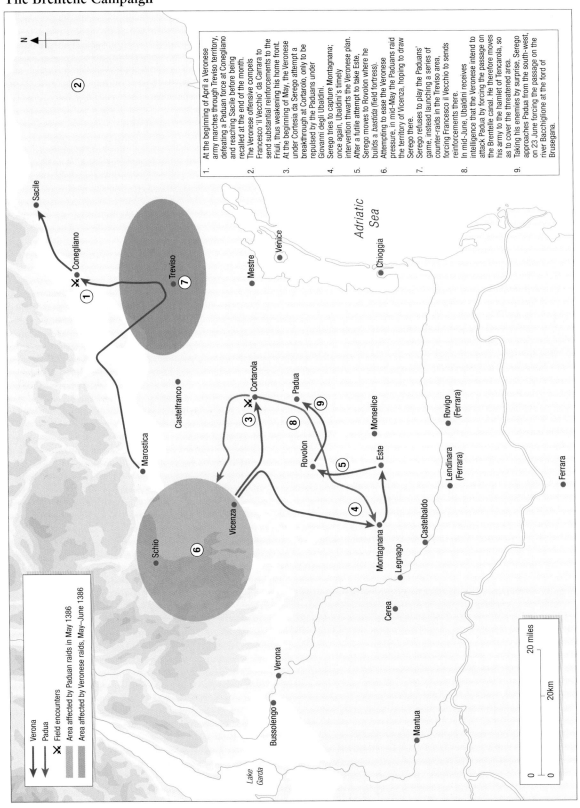

1. At the beginning of April a Veronese army marches through Treviso territory, defeating a Paduan force at Conegliano and reaching Sacile before being recalled at the end of the month.

2. The Veronese offensive compels Francesco 'il Vecchio' da Carrara to send substantial reinforcements to the Friuli, thus weakening his home front. At the beginning of May, the Veronese under Cortesia da Serego attempt a breakthrough at Cortarolo, only to be repulsed by the Paduans under Giovanni degli Ubaldini.

3. Serego tries to capture Montagnana; once again, Ubaldini's timely intervention thwarts the Veronese plan. After a futile attempt to take Este, Serego moves to Rovolon where he builds a *bastida* (field fortress).

4. Attempting to ease the Veronese pressure, in mid-May the Paduans raid the territory of Vicenza, hoping to draw Serego there.

5. Serego refuses to play the Paduans' game, instead launching a series of counter-raids in the Treviso area, forcing Francesco il Vecchio to sends reinforcements there.

6. In mid-June, Ubaldini receives intelligence that the Veronese intend to attack Padua by forcing the passage on the Brentelle canal. He therefore moves his army to the hamlet of Tencarola, so as to cover the threatened area.

7. Taking his enemies by surprise, Serego approaches Padua from the south-west, on 23 June forcing the passage on the river Bacchiglione at the ford of Brusegana.

38

in the Friuli, on 16 April, during the fording of the river Piave losing about 30 infantrymen captured by the Paduan garrison of Treviso. Carrara's troops – 250 lances, 150 infantry and 40 Hungarian cavalry – were at Conegliano, intending to block the enemy advance. With no other alternatives, the Veronese commanders, Ostasio da Polenta, Giovanni degli Ordelaffi and Gualtiero Borgognone, decided to fight it out. Initially the clash favoured the Paduans, their cavalry smashing into the Veronese horsemen and capturing many. As the Paduans engaged in rounding up their prisoners, the Veronese infantry counter-attacked and tipped the scales of the battle, sending Carrara's troops fleeing back into Conegliano. Casualties were minimal, only a few on both sides slain. With the road now open, the Veronese pushed on to Sacile, where in the following days they were joined by substantial reinforcements.

Depicted in this illumination, a number of soldiers riding out of a fortification. Although armoured in plate on their arms and elbows, mail aventails and bascinets, the illuminator of this scene from Sercambi's *Le croniche di Lucca* may intend these to represent the town's militia as they accompany wealthy but unarmed townspeople. (Archivio di Stato di Lucca, Ms 107, f. 130v. Authorisation 87/19. Su concessione del Ministero dei Beni e delle Attività Culturali e del Turismo. Duplicazione e riproduzione vietata con qualsiasi mezzo)

Suddenly, on 21 April, the whole army was recalled home, reaching Marostica a few days later after an uneventful march. Della Scala's decision baffled contemporaries and angered the Venetians, who were counting on the Veronese to support them in their fight for the Patriarchy of Aquileia. However, the lord of Verona had some very sound reasons to pull out of the Friuli. For one, he feared leaving his territories unguarded against Paduan raids. Second, his expedition in the Friuli had sufficiently alarmed Francesco il Vecchio, forcing him to increase his troops in the Friuli to 1,000 cavalry, thus weakening his army protecting Padua.

Probably around this time, Antonio Della Scala staged a *coup de théâtre* by challenging Francesco il Vecchio to a trial by combat – quite a normal occurrence in the chivalric world and mainly done for propaganda reasons, although as a counterpropaganda move Galeazo Gatari would lambaste Antonio as 'motivated by furore and evident folly'. Francesco Novello was willing to take up the challenge in his father's name, but the elder Carrara dismissed the suggestion outright with the words: 'Son, it is neither right nor honourable, that you and I, who are born of noble and legitimate matrimony, should fight with a most unworthy bastard, born from the stomach of a most base baker woman'. Francesco il Vecchio, however, knew better than to bring up illegitimacy of birth in diplomatic exchanges (the Carrara, after all, had their own share of bastards), answering the Veronese ambassador instead: 'You may tell your master Antonio Della Scala that since his great wickedness and ingratitude towards me is clear and that he does in no way desire peace, we have no intention to imperil our state but for sure we'll undo his'.

War began anew in early May, with the Veronese attempting to force an entry into Paduan territory, only to be repulsed thanks to the vigilance of the recently hired Giovanni degli Ubaldini. The Veronese then moved direction of attack, besieging 'with many bombards' the Paduan stronghold of Montagnana. Again, Ubaldini's timely intervention forced Della Scala to retreat. After another useless attempt against the town of Este, the Veronese

Plate armour for the hands developed a century before the battle of Castagnaro. Several steel plates covered the wrists and tops of the hands, with smaller plates sewn to the fingers of gloves. They had changed little since, although the plates had become fewer, three in this gauntlet from the Metropolitan Museum of Art. (The Metropolitan Museum of Art, New York)

shifted their attack to the west of Padua by building a *bastida* (field fortification) near Rovolon, from where they launched constant raids into enemy territory. The Paduans, in the meantime, had not been idle: the veteran captain and Florentine exile Bernardo degli Scolari raided as far as Schio. By threatening Della Scala's lands, the Paduans were trying to relieve pressure on their own, forcing the Veronese to move their troops nearer to home. However, their commander, Cortesia da Serego, did not take the bait, raiding instead the area around Treviso and compelling Carrara to send reinforcements there. Serego's strategy was to keep the Paduans guessing where he would strike next, forcing them to disperse their troops to protect key strategic locations.

Around mid-June, Carrara's intelligence managed to discover that Serego was planning to attack Padua from the west, forcing the passage on the Brentelle canal. To block the Veronese, Ubaldini moved most of his forces to Tencarola, on the Bacchiglione, in order to cover the main access routes to the city from that direction. Craving more information, he sent scouts there, only to discover that the Veronese camp had been struck. One of the locals told them that Serego was marching to the Brentelle. Immediately, Ubaldini brought his troops to the threatened area and ordered Jacopo da Carrara, Francesco il Vecchio's illegitimate son, to move his soldiers to the passage on the Brentelle. Undeterred, Serego made several feints in order to leave Ubaldini and Jacopo in the dark about his real objective, meanwhile torching the Paduan countryside. The refugees flowing into Padua put a strain on the city's resources, thus reducing its ability to sustain a prolonged siege.

But Serego was looking to attack rather than besiege Padua. Taking the Paduans by surprise, on 23 June he first marched south, to cross the

The Paduan town of Montagnana received its 2km circuit of walls in the 11th century. From then throughout the Middle Ages it served as a strongly fortified outpost where Paduan armies could seek refuge. Its walls withstood even the attack of Veronese bombards in May 1386. (Author's Collection)

This 14th-century illumination from the *Chronica de Carrarensibus* (Venice, Biblioteca Nazionale Marciana Lat X 381 f 1v) records the incident said to have begun the Padua–Veronese conflict. In 1237 Ezzelino III da Romano (*podesta* of Verona) insulted Jacopo da Carrara (a leading magnate in Padua) in the presence of Emperor Frederick II, only to receive a slap in return. The Emperor was forced to separate the two of them, but this did not stop Ezzelino from besieging Jacopo, with the Paduan dying trying to escape. (De Agostini Picture Library/Bridgeman Images)

Bacchiglione, then to the north placing his army just outside of the city in full view of those on the walls. With the shouts '*Scala! Scala!*', the Veronese taunted them, while Serego unveiled his gunpowder artillery. It was a psychological trick to instil fear into the enemy. Outnumbered, Ubaldini and Jacopo managed to retreat west into Padua, leaving it again, however, by the Santa Croce gate in the south. Serego had foolishly left no guard in this area, and, without hindrance, here the Paduan leaders regrouped their troops, soon to be joined by a substantial force under Pagano da Rho, who hastily managed to arrive from the south-west, avoiding the Veronese army.

Thinking he had won, Serego sent news to Verona about the successful operation, which produced much rejoicing and festive bonfires there and in Vicenza. An elated Antonio Della Scala started preparations to join his army, convinced that final victory over Carrara was but days away. His convictions were further strengthened by the astrologer Prezio di Monte Altino, who predicted that the Veronese troops would enter Padua. 'But' – would comment Andrea Gatari – 'Fortune, which sways the world's affairs in a manner distant from human desires and often causes those who initially laughed to cry in the end, decided to regulate matters differently'.

Serego intended to finish his business before the Paduans could receive any more reinforcements. Unfortunately for him, the next day torrential rain stopped all military operations. Francesco il Vecchio used this lull to order all men capable of bearing arms to gather on the city's main square, the muster amounting to 17,000 according to Andrea Gatari. Although this number may be an exaggeration, it might also take into account the large number of country folk who had poured into the city as refugees. Of these, Carrara chose about 6,000 men, quite possibly because he did not have enough equipment to arm more. He also prepared numerous carts of food, wine and weapons for his troops, with the added encouragement of the prediction

The Battle of Brentelle

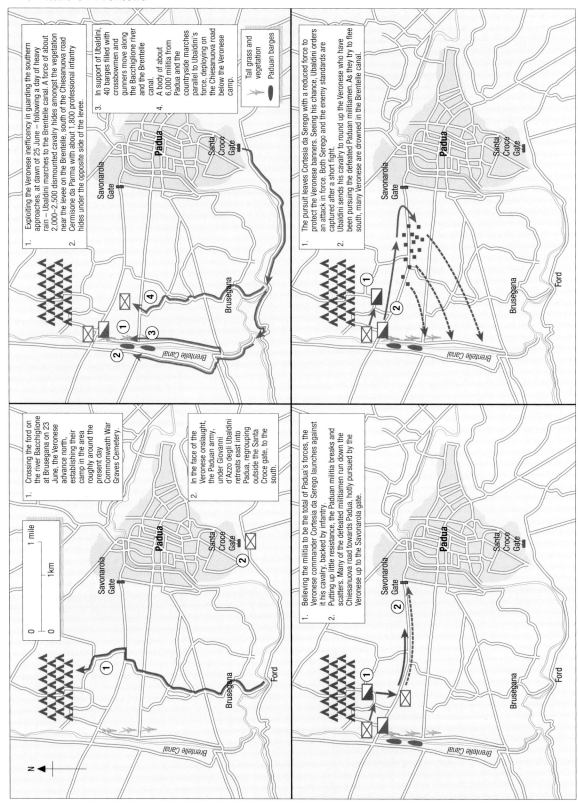

1. Exploiting the Veronese inefficiency in guarding the southern approaches, at dawn of 25 June – following a day of heavy rain – Ubaldini marches to the Brentelle canal. A force of about 2,000–2,500 dismounted cavalry hides amongst the vegetation near the levee on the Brentelle, south of the Chiesanuova road

2. Cermisone da Parma with about 1,800 professional infantry hides under the opposite side of the levee.

3. In support of Ubaldini, 40 barges filled with crossbowmen and gunners move along the Bacchiglione river and the Brentelle canal.

4. A body of about 6,000 militia from Padua and the countryside marches parallel to Ubaldini's force, deploying on the Chiesanuova road below the Veronese camp.

Key:
- Tall grass and vegetation
- Paduan barges

1. The pursuit leaves Cortesia da Serego with a reduced force to protect the Veronese banners. Seeing his chance, Ubaldini orders an attack in force. Both Serego and the enemy standards are captured after a short fight.

2. Ubaldini sends his cavalry to round up the Veronese who have been pursuing the defeated Paduan militiamen. As they try to flee south, many Veronese are drowned in the Brentelle canal.

1. Crossing the ford on the river Bacchiglione at Brusegana on 23 June, the Veronese advance north, establishing their camp in the area roughly around the present day Commonwealth War Graves Cemetery.

2. In the face of the Veronese onslaught, the Paduan army, under Giovanni d'Azzo degli Ubaldini retreats east into Padua, regrouping outside the Santa Croce gate, to the south.

1. Believing the militia to be the total of Padua's forces, the Veronese commander Cortesia da Serego launches against it his cavalry, backed by infantry.

2. Putting up little resistance, the Paduan militia breaks and scatters. Many of the defeated militiamen run down the Chiesanuova road towards Padua, hotly pursued by the Veronese up to the Savonarola gate.

42

made by the astrologer Bonifacio Pellacani: should the Paduans engage the enemy, they would surely be victorious and bring many prisoners into the city. Thus, even before it was fought on the field, the battle had been fought among the stars, the reputation of two city lords and of two seers closely entwined.

Ubaldini, meanwhile, was relying on other signs than those from the skies. He had a plan – a risky endeavour, but if successful it would reap great dividends. Ubaldini counted on Serego's overconfidence, the Veronese certain of victory. Too sure, as a matter of fact, to guard the Brentelle canal, where on the night of 24–25 June under the cover of the rain 40 barges filled with Paduan troops, 'gunners and crossbowmen', moved up to the levee near an area known as i Taglidi. The following morning, Ubaldini gave a prep speech to his troops, among other things promising double pay for victory. Then he silently led his force of about 2,000–2,500 dismounted cavalry and 1,800 infantry, under Cermisone da Parma, towards the levee, using it as a screen to hide his movements. Once Ubaldini had reached a spot that allowed him to observe the Veronese without being detected, he ordered his soldiers to lay down on the grass and wait.

As planned by Ubaldini, the Paduan militia with the supply carts advanced towards the ford at the Brentelle. It did not take long for the Veronese to spot them and Serego marvelled that he was facing an army of peasants. Nevertheless, he ordered his men to arms, dividing the cavalry into 14 units and ordering the two under Francesco da Sassuolo and the redoubtable Facino Cane to attack. Their mounted charge pushed back the militia, who, however, did not break, forcing Serego to feed more troops into the battle. After a while, the cavalry under Ostasio da Polenta aided by Veronese infantry managed to drive a wedge within the enemy ranks. As their cohesion collapsed, the militia fled for their lives. Many ran towards the Savonarola gate, chased by the victors shouting 'Scala! Scala!'. Serego sent a number of his squadrons (*squadre*) to chase the fugitives but, seeing the baggage train, Veronese discipline disappeared in a flurry of disorderly looting.

This did not bother Serego, who immediately sent a message to Antonio Della Scala informing him of the great victory, convinced he had beaten the Paduans. Entirely different was Francesco il Vecchio's reaction when some of the survivors who had managed to enter the city arrived with the news of the Veronese success. According to Galeazzo Gatari: 'driven by ire, he removed several times his hat and slammed it on the chair in the court under the chancery lodge, in rage gnawing and drooling over the rod he held in his hand'. Andrea Gatari, writing many years later and with nostalgia for bygone days, gives us a rather more dignified picture of the elder Carrara on hearing about the debacle: 'his face became ashen, but immediately he recomposed himself and mounting on horseback went to the square to encourage his people and his citizens'.

In another detail from the altar of St James in the Cathedral of St Zeno in Pistoia a group of soldiers stands behind St James as he is being questioned by Herod. These soldiers wear bascinets and a combination of plate and mail armours. The central figure, perhaps the captain, has a metal breastplate with overlapping metal plates (faulds) descending down the front as well as a mail aventail attached to his bascinet. (Photo by DeAgostini/Getty Images)

On the field, Ubaldini had quite a different reaction. On hearing clamour of the Paduan rout he took to the saddle to have a better view and noticed Serego in the company of 'but few people' – probably the 'armoured horsemen with lances' cited in the above-mentioned list, mounted *provisionati* of Scala's household troops and recruited among the prominent citizens of Verona and Vicenza. Realizing that he now had an advantage, Ubaldini went for the jugular. Trumpets passed on the order to mount. Ubaldini informed his commanders that he intended to go 'for the Scala banners' and ordered Cermisone to strike the Veronese flank. Raising high the baton of command, Ubaldini shouted: '*Mongioia, viva il Carro*!' receiving in answer a raucous '*Carro, Carro*!' – a reference to the Carrara coat-of-arms – as the Paduans broke cover charging into the midst of the enemy.

Caught completely by surprise, Serego managed nevertheless to face the attackers. It was too little, too late as Paduan lances started emptying Veronese saddles. Conte da Carrara, another of Francesco il Vecchio's illegitimate sons, with a group of men-at-arms, pulled the Veronese standard-bearer from his horse and wrenched from him the Scala banner. Cermisone's infantry hitting the Veronese flank closed the matter for good, Serego and all his men forced to surrender. The indefatigable Ubaldini then turned to the road, sweeping from it the Veronese who had stopped to pillage the baggage. Seeing their leaders captured, these abandoned prisoners and booty, taking flight. Many were forced to surrender, while others drowned trying to cross the Brentelle, their escape route south blocked by the barged-in Paduan gunners and crossbowmen. 'Thus', writes Galeazzo Gatari 'in less than two hours they [the Veronese] were defeated and captured in a body, together with their wagons, tents and huts'.

Despite Gatari's account, a certain amount of Veronese managed to escape the field. According to a much later source, one of Serego's sergeants encountered Antonio Della Scala at the head of 400 horsemen en route for what he believed to be his triumphal entry into Padua. While still at a distance, the frantic soldier shouted: 'Go back, my lord, for your army is destroyed'. It did not take long for the stunned Antonio to receive a more detailed report from other stragglers, including the news of Serego's capture.

Two infantry armies clash in an illumination from Sercambi's *La croniche di Lucca*. Almost all wear open-faced bascinets with mail aventails, as well as a mixture of mail and plate armours covering arms and legs – torso armours are obscured by tunics, round shields and pavises. Spears are their most common weapon. (Archivio di Stato di Lucca, Ms 107, f. 134r. Authorisation 87/19. Su concessione del Ministero dei Beni e delle Attività Culturali e del Turismo. Duplicazione e riproduzione vietata con qualsiasi mezzo)

Hastily he returned to Vicenza and then to Verona, where the populace had already made preparations to celebrate a great victory. However, once the bitter tidings became known, the joy quickly turned 'into sadness and pain'.

The opposite was true in Padua. A beaming Francesco il Vecchio immediately had Ubaldini and five other commanders dubbed as knights. Then he ordered the victorious troops and the prisoners to parade through Padua and, on meeting Serego, accompanied by Ubaldini, he greeted him in a half-mocking way with the words: 'You are bestowing on us a great honour with your visit, but our thanks and the merit for this go to our Captain-General'. Serego simply answered: 'Magnificent lord, it is but the practice of war'. Also captured were 48 senior and junior officers, plus 9,460 men 'of all social conditions'. The total of those slain during the battle or drowned in the Brentelle came to 521, whom Carrara ordered buried in nearby churches. The booty from the Veronese camp included 6,353 warhorses and 211 prostitutes, the latter richly feted at the lord of Padua's table. Considering that, according to one source, Serego had started the battle with 7,000 horsemen, from a military and logistical standpoint the defeat at the Brentelle had been a major debacle for Della Scala.

The Brentelle canal as it is today. Somewhere near here, on 25 June 1386, the Paduans (mostly militia) defeated the Veronese. The victory brought a large amount of booty to the city, but 521 of the Paduans were killed. (Author's Collection)

The Veronese prisoners of rank were allowed the option to ransom themselves or switch sides. Among those who chose the latter were Facino Cane and his brother Filippino. Furious about the Cane brothers' defection, Della Scala could do little else but have them hanged in effigy in Verona. The other captives were freed as their ransom money arrived, on condition that they did not take up arms against Padua in the two months following their release. Serego, however, was not treated so leniently and only liberated more than a year later, after agreeing to pay 9,000 ducats in ransom. Worn down by the long imprisonment, the defeated Veronese commander died of fever sometime in late 1387.

BROTHERS-IN-LAW

From Milan, Gian Galeazzo Visconti had been watching with keen eyes the political and military developments. Immediately after the defeat at the Brentelle, the Count of Virtue sent a delegation to Verona offering condolences and armed support, if so desired, to exact revenge on the Paduans. At the same time, however, Visconti was proposing to Francesco il Vecchio a Paduan-Milanese alliance against Verona! Galeazzo Gatari would acidly comment about Gian Galeazzo's 'fraudulent' behaviour: 'Thus the Count of Virtue played with two cloaks at one time'. Given Visconti's reputation for treachery, Gatari was being somewhat euphemistic in his statement.

Carrara was more inclined to pursue peace talks with Della Scala rather than pursue Visconti's offer. Despite the victory at the Brentelle,

In an anonymous painting dating c.1405, and now in the Metropolitan Museum of Art, St Michael is dressed in the armour of a well-to-do knight. Plates cover the front of his legs and his entire arms. He also wears plate gauntlets and articulated sabatons (on his feet). His torso is protected by a brigandine, the rivets attached to plates inside. He carries a buckler in his left hand while wielding a hand-and-a-half sword in his right, about to deliver a killing blow to a dragon. (The Metropolitan Museum of Art, New York)

the war had been financially, materially and politically costly. Even an ambitious and avaricious individual like Francesco il Vecchio realized that should this situation continue, the survival of his regime would be at risk. Therefore, immediately after the Brentelle he sent an embassy to Verona with a peace proposition. Della Scala was even worse off than his adversary, having all of Carrara's problems plus a weakened military capacity after the recent disaster. Yet, conflicting opinions existed among his advisers, some advocating peace and others pushing for continuing the conflict. The scales were tipped by 60,000 ducats from Venice as a contribution to Della Scala's war effort and the Paduan embassy went home empty handed. The Venetians were more than happy to see the Paduans and the Veronese bleed each other to death, while peace between the two city-states would have meant Carrara unleashing his full military force into the Friuli – for Venice a veritable nightmare.

Even before being rebuffed on the diplomatic front, at the end of June the Paduans returned to war, Ubaldini devastating the countryside around Verona. He then turned against the dam diverting the Bacchiglione, overcoming the defenders after a fierce fight and restoring the water supply for Padua's mills. The Veronese *bastida* at Rovolon was his next objective, taking it in August and putting there a Paduan garrison. At the end of July, a surprise Paduan attack aided by treason stormed a still unfinished Veronese *bastida* at Montecchio Precalcino, north of Vicenza, burning it to the ground. Soon after, the Veronese had the satisfaction of catching the turncoat responsible for the deed and, fittingly, executed him by slowly roasting him on a spit in the Campo Marzio of Vicenza.

Despite all this, Della Scala had not been idle. Thanks to Venetian money and the liberation of some of his senior commanders captured at the Brentelle, he gradually rebuilt an army; soldiers were recruited in German-speaking territories and conveyed to the town of Sacile, while two other gathering points were established at Marostica and at Mestre, in Venetian territory. On 12 September the Veronese commander Giovanni degli Ordelaffi, recently released after being captured at the Brentelle, felt strong enough to go into action, conducting a two-day march through enemy territory from Marostica to Sacile, where the troops from Mestre were similarly expected. Once the whole Veronese army came together it amounted to 1,500 lances, 700 infantry and 200 crossbowmen, a strong fighting force poised to do significant damage to the nearby Carrara territories.

Ordelaffi, however, appears to have been just above average as a military leader and well below in exercising his authority. No sooner had his troops gathered, than a scuffle broke out between Italians and Germans that quickly developed into a full-scale battle. The Italians, superior in numbers, 'cut to pieces' many of their opponents and then proceeded 'to rob the aforesaid

Germans of all their weapons, horses and other belongings'. The survivors found refuge in nearby castles before crossing the Tagliamento River to the haven of Cividale, under Paduan control. Once there they elected a leader and wrote to Francesco il Vecchio offering their services. A delighted Carrara hired the lot. From Cividale the Germans launched raids against Venice and her allies in the Friuli, even managing to cut off the city of Udine's water supply.

After this inauspicious start, Ordelaffi lingered six days in Sacile. On 20 September he began marching back towards Vicenza, burning and looting on his way, at the head of 1,500 lances, 1,700 infantry, 400 crossbowmen and 500 Hungarian cavalry. The reason for this backtracking may have had to do with having unwittingly increased Padua's forces in the Friuli, but it is more likely that Della Scala had no intention of acting as Venice's proxy, his goal still Carrara's destruction.

Once Ordelaffi's troops reached their quarters in Marostica, they received a rude shock: the lord of Verona had hired a new commander-in-chief, the *condottiere*, Lutz von Landau, whose three-month contract included a company of 500 lances of 400 infantry. Lutz, the son of the celebrated Konrad von Landau, had a solid reputation as a reliable and able commander, thoroughly immersed in Italy's affairs. Yet, for many Italians he was still a *forestiere* – a foreigner – and the recent fight between Italians and Germans at Sacile had only increased this xenophobic attitude among Della Scala's troops. Thus, once they receive news of Landau's imminent arrival, several captains promptly abandoned Verona's service and went over to Carrara's, bringing with them 300 horsemen.

Undeterred by more defections, on 6 October Ordelaffi left Marostica, cutting a swathe of destruction through Treviso's countryside. Many farmers were caught unawares and captured while attending the grape harvest and the booty included hundreds of animals. Four days later Ordelaffi reached Landau's headquarters in Mestre, where he solemnly bestowed the baton of command to the German captain. Landau, however, was politically savvy enough to make Ordelaffi his deputy for all Italian troops, undoubtedly wishing to avoid another Sacile incident.

The Veronese army now amounted to 2,500 horsemen, 2,000 infantry, 'many Hungarian [mounted] archers' and a good number of crossbowmen, plus a large supply train. Getting back to base without being intercepted was a major problem now, Landau calculating that the Paduans would be guarding the road to Marostica through the Treviso countryside. He, therefore, in a counter-intuitive move, on 11 October marched west to then push south and – with the aid of bundles of straw – wade across the marshes created by the river Brenta near Sandon and then proceed to Piove di Sacco. By skirting Padua to the east and then push through Carrara territory at the ford near Castelbaldo, Landau surmised that he would

In this detail from the *Queste de Saint Graal* (c.1380–85) three Arthurian knights observe the death of Sir Perceval's sister. Plates cover the front of their legs, forearms, hands and feet; mail protects their upper arms. They wear visored bascinets with attached mail aventails, their visors raised. Sensing danger, the foremost knight reaches for his sword with the right hand while grasping his dagger with his left. (Bibliotheque Nationale, Paris, France/Archives Charmet/ Bridgeman Images)

This mid-14th-century ivory chess piece from the Metropolitan Museum of Art shows a knight riding straight-legged, apparently beginning a charge – his broken lance is raised. He wears metal plates on his legs and knees, but is otherwise covered in mail, as is his horse. His shield is ready for a blow, but his visor is raised on his bascinet, no doubt to be lowered before contact with an opponent. (The Metropolitan Museum of Art, New York)

be in Veronese lands before the Paduans realized what had happened and ransacking their countryside in the process. Unfortunately, his adversaries got wind of his intentions, and Landau found all the passages on the Brenta well guarded, forcing him to turn back.

Pitching his camp near Zero Branco, Landau sent out several raiding expeditions, his plan to mislead the Paduans about his real intentions and probe enemy defences. These came back loaded with booty and captives, the Paduans too busy defending the passages on the Brenta to counter the threat north. Landau struck camp on 14 October crossing the river Sile, and two days later appearing in front of the Paduan *bastida* at Onigo. The fort's defenders were a substantial number and well provided but with little fighting spirit, quickly surrendering. Landau ordered the *bastida* destroyed before moving on, pillaging the countryside before returning to Vicenza on the 26th. His campaign had exposed the Paduans' military weakness in Friuli and the Treviso area, forcing Francesco il Vecchio to send some 500 horsemen there. Lutz had confirmed his reputation as a master strategist.

No sooner had Landau returned to Vicenza than he received Della Scala's order to capture the fortifications the Paduans had erected to stop the Bacchiglione from again being diverted. The German captain marched out of Vicenza with bombards in his train on 30 October, managing to outfox Francesco Novello by making him believe he intended to strike elsewhere. Once Lutz arrived at the Paduan 'towers', he set to work to isolate them by building ditches and levees and subjecting the fortifications to intense artillery barrage. To counter this, Francesco il Vecchio ordered Ubaldini to raid deep into Veronese territory, hoping to force Landau into lifting his sieges. Lutz was too shrewd a strategist to take the bait, opting instead for a counter-raid into Paduan lands. He managed to get as far as 10km north of Padua, where he encountered a force sent to intercept him under Francesco Novello and Bernardo degli Scolari. From the few details available, it would appear that the encounter was brief and violent; and even if Landau was forced to retire, news circulated that the younger Carrara had been captured: 'but, thank God, this proved untrue'. It is hard not to see in the older Gatari's praise to deity a criticism of Francesco Novello, whose known recklessness presumably had caused him to take greater personal risks than warranted.

Despite the reverse, Landau still held the strategic initiative and, moreover, the Paduans had been unable to pull the Veronese away from their beleaguered 'towers'. On the evening of 25 November, a force of 1,000 lances under Ubaldini, Biancardo, Scolari and Ugolino Ghisleri rode out of Padua, with three carts loaded with bolts, guns and gunpowder, plus another cart carrying a boat. Deftly evading Veronese lookouts, at nightfall the Paduans were in position upstream from the 'towers'. Loading the boat with the equipment, they managed to reach the fortifications undetected; a second trip brought further reinforcements of 50 infantry. No sooner had the men and *matériel* arrived than the defenders started shouting: '*Carro, Carro, battaglia, battaglia!*' and firing their artillery against the enemy camp. Veronese trumpets sounded, and the besiegers rushed to their positions, the ensuing commotion allowing Ubaldini and the others to exfiltrate unseen.

The relief of the 'towers' would prove short lived. The Veronese, furious about having been tricked, intensified their bombard fire, reducing the 'towers' to rubble and forcing the defenders to hide in underground tunnels. The surviving Paduans finally surrendered on 7 December, 'saving their lives and belongings'. Immediately, the Veronese set to work to divert the Bacchiglione and deny Padua's mills of their water supply. Raids and counter-raids followed, but the Paduans could not keep the Veronese from cutting several supply routes to their city.

In an attempt to remove the problem, Francesco il Vecchio resorted to a trick that had worked so many times with mercenaries: bribery. Knowing that Landau's three-month contract with Della Scala was about to expire, sometime in December Carrara offered 10,000 ducats, should he promise not to serve the Veronese for six months after leaving their service. Covertly he was trying to get Landau to switch sides. On reception, Lutz – 'being a good and loyal individual', as Galeazzo Gatari would comment, not without irony – immediately showed the letter to Della Scala, in the hope of a counter-offer. Della Scala, however, arrogantly told Landau he could freely accept Carrara's proposal, 'since winter is approaching and we can perform well enough without your services for the next six months'. A resentful Landau shot back: 'Watch your regime closely, for as soon as I depart you'll surely find the Paduan army at your doorstep'. Unimpressed, Della Scala retorted: 'We have the means to defend ourselves. Take his [Carrara's] money, for then he'll have less for other needs'.

Della Scala's decision to dismiss Landau was seen at the time as foolhardy, given that in less than three months the German captain had nullified the Paduans' strategic advantage after the Brentelle. Antonio might simply have been running out of cash and did not have the funds to retain Landau; yet, Verona's military effort in the next months would appear to contradict such an assumption. Della Scala might also have been bowing to the resentment of his Italian *condottieri* against a foreigner, coupled with the political and military ambitions of his brother-in-law Ostasio da Polenta. Whichever the case, Lutz left Verona's service at the end of December, duly receiving his 10,000 ducats from Carrara.

Francesco il Vecchio had, in the meantime, landed a major coup by enlisting Landau's brother-in-law, Sir John Hawkwood. Since his return from the Neapolitan campaign the English captain had been one of the leaders of a freebooting mercenary company, which engaged in a short spell of extortion mainly at the expense of Perugia and Lucca. In the summer of 1385 he had signed a *condotta in aspetto* (roughly a 'suspended contract') with Gian Galeazzo Visconti with the promise to serve when needed, the Florentines, with whom Hawkwood had a similar agreement, giving their tacit approval to the deal. Thus, Sir John was collecting money by sitting idly in his Tuscan estates and engaging in diplomatic activities on behalf of Richard II of England. He had also transformed his estate

Trumpets (known as buisines), such as these in a 15th-century illumination celebrating the marriage of Francesco Sforza and Bianca Maria Visconti in 1441, were used by armies on late medieval battlefields to communicate commands, their sounds one of the few things able to be heard over the din of fighting. (Photo by DeAgostini/ Getty Images)

of Montecchio Vesponi into a haven for fellow English mercenaries, a convenient way to have reliable soldiers at the ready when needed.

Still, indolence hardly appealed to a man of action, although now in his mid-60s but still physically and mentally agile. Besides, his military reputation depended heavily on his taking the field, as witnessed by a famous anecdote reported by the contemporary Florentine novelist Franco Sacchetti. Around this time, while staying in Montecchio, Hawkwood received the visit of two Franciscan friars on a collection mission. '*Monsignore*, may God grant you peace', they greeted Sir John, to which he shot back: 'May God take away your alms!' 'Sir, why do you say thus?' asked the somewhat intimidated friars. 'Then why did you speak to me in that manner?' responded the Englishman. 'We thought to have spoken appropriately', the befuddled clerics excused themselves. 'Appropriately?' snapped Hawkwood. 'How can you say that by wishing that God make me starve to death? Don't you know that I make my living with war and peace would utterly ruin me? So, war is my livelihood as for your alms; thus my answer reflected your greeting'. At this the two friars shrugged their shoulders, simply saying: 'Sir you are right. Forgive us for we are ignorant people'. 'And' Sacchetti would add 'this was a fine and new tale; especially for what concerns Sir John Hawkwood, but not for those who would have wanted to live in peace'.

True or not, Sacchetti's story is testimony of Hawkwood's restlessness caused by his inactivity. Therefore, when he was approached by Ubaldini on behalf of Francesco il Vecchio, he leapt at the chance. Hawkwood accepted around the end of December a contract for 500 lances and 500 archers, his agreement with Carrara enjoying also the tacit backing of both the Florentine government and Visconti.

It would take time for Sir John to put his company together, the composition of which is a matter of speculation. While we can be pretty sure that the archers were all from Hawkwood's native country, we cannot

Most of medieval soldiers' lives was spent in non-military activities. If they were militia, they returned to their normal occupations and lives. Professional soldiers, however, were only soldiers. Keeping them busy was a difficult task for their captains, who knew that bored soldiers, especially mercenaries, might create problems. Gambling was a frequent distraction. These dice-playing soldiers are from a Crucifixion scene in an Italian Missal of the period (Bibliothèque nationale de France. Département des manuscrits. Français 343)

be so certain about his men-at-arms. Undoubtedly the majority were from England – Sir John keeping close ties with his fellow countrymen in Italy – on the other hand, over the years Hawkwood had often bonded with German and Italian mercenaries, so it is not impossible to think that a few of these made their way into Sir John's retinue. They were all reliable men, tested in warfare and loyal to their commander.

While Hawkwood was gathering his troops, the military situation in the north was witnessing new developments. Landau's departure had not halted the Veronese offensive. On 15 January 1387 Della Scala's troops captured the Covolo of the Brenta, a fortified cave on the road to Feltre. According to the chronicler Conforto da Costozza, the stronghold was taken thanks to the use of bombards firing 'fiery balls and other malodorous concoctions and these burning with stench ravaged those inside, who [surrendered] saving their life and possessions', with Costozza further informing us that these devices had been invented by one Sbrega, an apothecary from Vicenza. The taking of the Covolo was yet another

The Castagnaro Campaign

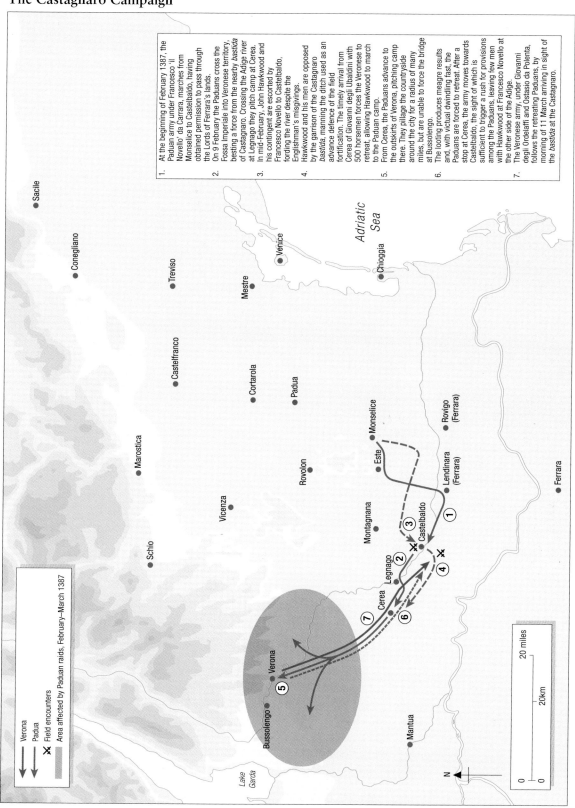

1. At the beginning of February 1387, the Paduan army under Francesco 'il Novello' da Carrara, marches from Monselice to Castelbaldo, having obtained permission to pass through the Lords of Ferrara's lands.

2. On 9 February the Paduans cross the Fossa Imperiale into Veronese territory, besting a force from the nearby *bastida* of Castagnaro. Crossing the Adige river at Legnago they pitch camp at Cerea. In mid-February, John Hawkwood and his contingent are escorted by Francesco Novello to Castelbaldo, fording the river despite the Englishman's misgivings.

3. Hawkwood and his men are opposed by the garrison of the Castagnaro *bastida*, manning the ditch used as an advance defence of the field fortification. The timely arrival from Cerea of Giovanni degli Ubaldini with 500 horsemen forces the Veronese to retreat, allowing Hawkwood to march to the Paduan camp.

4. From Cerea, the Paduans advance to the outskirts of Verona, pitching camp there. They pillage the countryside around the city for a radius of many miles, but are unable to force the bridge at Bussolengo.

5. The looting produces meagre results and, with victual dwindling fast, the Paduans are forced to retreat. After a stop at Cerea, the army moves towards Castelbaldo, the sight of which is sufficient to trigger a rush for provisions among the Paduans, leaving few men with Hawkwood at Francesco Novello at the other side of the Adige.

6. The Veronese army, under Giovanni degli Ordelaffi and Ostasio da Polenta, follows the retreating Paduans, by morning of 11 March arriving in sight of the *bastida* at the Castagnaro.

Verona
Padua
✕ Field encounters
Area affected by Paduan raids, February–March 1387

Lake Garda

Sacile

Conegliano

Treviso

Mestre

Venice

Adriatic Sea

Chioggia

Castelfranco

Cortarola

Padua

Marostica

Rovolon

Monselice

Este

Rovigo (Ferrara)

Vicenza

Montagnana

Lendinara (Ferrara)

Schio

Legnago

Castelbaldo

Cerea

Bussolengo

Verona

Mantua

Ferrara

N

20 miles
20km

building block in the Veronese strategy for isolating Padua by cutting off its communication routes, before making another attempt to finish the job brusquely interrupted at the Brentelle.

Desperate to stall the Veronese offensive, Francesco il Vecchio decided to launch a raid in force across the Adige River into Della Scala's lands. Ubaldini had misgivings about the soundness of such an operation but was forced to obey orders. For the sake of maximum surprise, the plan called for a march from Monselice to Castelbaldo and from there crossing into Veronese territory before the enemy had time to realize what was happening. However, this meant passing through the lands of the lords of Ferrara and initial requests for the Paduan army's transit were politely refused, the Este, although ostensibly allies of the Carrara, not wishing to get embroiled in the ongoing conflict. Francesco Novello took matters into his own hands by badgering his father-in-law, Niccolò d'Este, grudgingly to give permission.

The Paduan forces under Ubaldini and Francesco Novello gathered in Monselice in the first days of February, marching to Castelbaldo via the Ferrarese stronghold of Lendinara; on 9 February 1387 the army entered Veronese territory through the Fossa Imperiale, a deep ditch some 3km north-west of Castelbaldo. The crossing did not go unopposed, the Veronese engaging the invaders in a sharp fight before being forced to the nearby *bastida* of the Castagnaro. This fortification represents a minor mystery, its existence confirmed by different sources but its exact location unknown. With the evidence available we can speculate it stood at the junction between the Adige and the Castagnaro canal, on the opposite bank from the Fossa Imperiale, to control the river traffic. It probably also overlooked a ford, which would explain how the Veronese managed to retreat with relative ease to the *bastida* across the Adige – the waters low before the spring thaw in the Alps caused them to rise.

Following the course of the Adige upstream, the Paduans crossed it at Legnago, from there marching 8km west to Cerea. Once they established camp there, together with the familiar pattern of raiding the surrounding countryside, Francesco Novello left Ubaldini in charge and rode off towards Monselice to greet some very important guests.

TURNIPS, HORSEMEAT AND ARTILLERY

Hawkwood had arrived in Carrara territory at about the same time the Paduans launched their invasion against Verona, with him Giovanni Tarlati da Pietramala – known as Tedesco – a rising star in the mercenary profession. Both Sir John and Pietramala had travelled to Padua, where they had been lavishly entertained by Francesco il Vecchio before returning to their troops billeted in Monselice. There they met Francesco Novello to whom they communicated his father's orders to cross the Fossa Imperiale and from there reach the Paduan camp at Cerea, the army's march proceeding under falling rain. Once they reached Castelbaldo, however, Francesco Novello decided to cross the Adige there, whether because he considered it too risky trying to force the Fossa Imperiale or because of wanting to exercise full control over the expedition.

In times of peace the opposite banks of the Adige at Castelbaldo were connected by a pontoon bridge, which the Veronese had dismantled. Despite

Hawkwood's suggestion of taking a separate route, Francesco Novello insisted on crossing the river at a nearby ford. Once on the opposite bank the Paduans found their way blocked by the Veronese from the nearby *bastida* manning a deep and wide ditch, which had cost Della Scala a considerable sum. It ran from the Adige levee to a swamp created by the overflowing of the Castagnaro, an advanced defence of the *bastida* against potential invaders from the direction of Castelbaldo. Ubaldini had somehow got news of Francesco Novello's intentions and dispatched to the ditch a relief force of 500 horse. Caught between these two armies, the Veronese retreated to the *bastida*, allowing the Paduans to reach Cerea 'where that night they rested the best they could in bitter cold'.

The next morning Francesco Novello called a war council to discuss further strategy. The senior Paduan commanders listened as he complained that 'our men are doing nothing here' and advocating an advance deep into Veronese territory, asking for everyone's opinion on the matter. All looked at each other inquisitively and in silence until Hawkwood turned to Ubaldini and asked: 'My lord captain, will you not answer?' Ubaldini then stood up holding his baton of command and addressing Francesco Novello solemnly stated that he would not dare speak before Sir John, 'despite the fact that I still hold the honourable baton of command of your Carrara army'. Then, with a sudden *coup de théâtre*, he submitted his resignation, suggesting Hawkwood take his place. Faced with a fait accompli, Hawkwood could do nothing but graciously accept the offer, although he insisted he and Ubaldini share leadership. Sir John then endorsed Francesco Novello's proposal and the Paduan army proceeded to strike camp.

Ubaldini's apparent modesty cannot be considered completely selfless. While his deference towards Hawkwood was for the most part genuine, by passing on the baton Ubaldini had removed a considerable burden from his shoulders, although officially Padua's captain-general, Francesco Novello's presence largely negated his authority. Besides, Ubaldini had no backing from any state, having been forced into exile by the Florentines who had also put a price on his head. Hawkwood, on the other hand, enjoyed the support of both Florence and Milan, and was therefore more likely to stand up, if necessary, to the whims of the younger or elder Carrara. Still, Sir John was astute enough to insist on shared leadership with Ubaldini, the latter's presence going a long way in defusing any sort of tension that might arise among Italians troops on receiving orders from a *forestiero*.

The Paduan army advanced to the gates of Verona, burning, looting and taking prisoners on its way. The Veronese under Polenta and Ordelaffi shadowed at a distance, harassing the enemy with constant skirmishing. The Paduan raiding parties inflicted terrible damage on Della Scala's lands. Yet, despite the plundering of the countryside, the loot was turning out far less than expected, war having already taken its toll on agricultural production and the winter season leaving the land bare. Victuals in the Paduan camp

An illuminated 'B' from a Northern Italian manuscript of Lucan's *Pharsalia*, dating to the last quarter of the 14th century includes a soldier, probably a knight, dressed in a brigandine over a mail shirt. His helmet-less head is covered by a cap which could very well be an 'arming cap', what most knights would wear in between their hair and helmet. (British Library, Harley 2532, f. 1r)

This typical scene of St George's defeat of the dragon was painted by Altichiero da Zevo for St George's Oratory in Padua (finished in 1384). St George, always portrayed in the most up-to-date armour, is covered completely in steel plates, painted black (most itinerant knights would do so to prevent rusting), in what looks to be a fully integrated suit of armour, only then beginning to appear for purchase by the wealthiest warriors. He wears his shield on his back, and his visor is raised on his bascinet to better see as he thrusts at the reptile with his lance. (The Picture Art Collection/Alamy Stock Photo)

started to diminish, to the point that soldiers went without bread and meat for 20 days, according to Galeazzo Gatari, 'being reduced to eat legumes and turnips, while some cooked their own horses for want of food'.

In this predicament, the army leaders strove to put on a brave face, but in truth the supply situation was deteriorating by the day. The Paduans had penetrated too deep in enemy territory, miscalculating their capacity to live off the land. To make matters worse, the Veronese kept close watch on the roads to Padua, intercepting all the couriers sent by Francesco Novello to his father with requests for relief. The letters seized from the captured messengers gave Antonio Della Scala a pretty good idea of the enemy's situation, increasing his confidence and hopes that payback for the Brentelle was imminent.

Della Scala, however, decided to check for himself by sending one of his secretaries, by the name of Paliano, to Hawkwood and Ubaldini, with the request that they ask Francesco Novello to get his father to discuss peace talks. Paliano's mission, instead, was to assess the situation in the enemy camp and delay as long as possible to increase the Paduans' discomfiture, plus, even more important, discover if any deal existed between Francesco il Vecchio and Gian Galeazzo Visconti. The Count of Virtue had been promising the Veronese aid against the Paduans, but Della Scala suspected Visconti again 'to be playing with two cloaks' by seeking an agreement also with Padua at Verona's expense. Of course, Della Scala was correct, Gian Galeazzo's utter lack of scruples and morals was breathtaking even by contemporary Italian standards. Indeed, Visconti was already negotiating a possible alliance with Francesco il Vecchio, but Paliano could not find out anything concrete about the matter and returned to his master empty handed.

Still, Paliano confirmed the Paduan army to be in dire straits for lack of victuals and Della Scala decided it was high time to strike. Together with his military leaders – Giovanni degli Ordelaffi, Ostasio da Polenta and Benedetto da Malcesine – he formulated a plan of action. Antonio had made good the gap caused by the departure of Landau and his company by recruiting in Germany and Italy and also proclaimed a general levy in his territories. Yet the disaster at the Brentelle had clearly left Verona's weapon stocks depleted, since Antonio ordered large quantities of leaden maces 'for all those who requested one, so as to kill everyone in the Carrara army'.

Large bombards were manufactured, and large quantities of munitions and victuals gathered in preparation for the campaign, including the cart-mounted artillery that so impressed Galeazzo Gatari.

March had already entered its second week when the Paduan commanders finally realized that, to forestall dying of starvation, retreat was the only option. The decision was made to backtrack south to Castelbaldo. The only real obstacle was the enemy *bastida* at the Adige – Castagnaro junction, but the garrison there had proved unable to stop the Paduans during their advance and the Veronese lurking behind the *bastida*'s defences would have been courageous indeed in trying to block thousands of hungry, desperate men.

Probably on the morning of 8 March, the Paduan army started moving towards Castelbaldo, its march slowed by the muddy conditions of the roads because of the recent rains. Carrara's commanders had planned a logistical stop at Cerea, but once they reached it, the troops had the nasty surprise of finding all the wells and wine vats poisoned by the enemy. According to Galeazzo Gatari, Hawkwood solved the problem by using a special ring to purify the liquids. Andrea Gatari, Galeazzo's son, states that Sir John did not use a ring but instead the horn of a unicorn, 'five feet in length which I saw and touched with my very hands, and this he grated into many wells'. While easy to dismiss these wondrous stories as mere fables of a superstitious age, it is also possible that an experienced commander like Sir John used some sort of natural antidote as a purifier – maybe with a bit of theatre added – such remedies known thanks to widely read works, such as those of the ancient Greek physician Galen. It is also possible, as some have suggested, that not all the wells had been contaminated.

Fact or fiction notwithstanding, the poisoned water sources and wine stocks at Cerea did not stop the Paduans' retreat. In the meantime also, the Veronese army had started to move, but showed no haste to catch up with the enemy. Della Scala's commanders surmised, correctly as it would turn out, that once Carrara's troops reached the vicinity of Castelbaldo, anarchy would prevail as the hungry soldiers rushed the town in search of much-needed food 'and we shall easily beat them'. The information about supplies stocked inside Castelbaldo would indicate that, somehow, Francesco Novello had managed to inform his father of his army's predicament, but is also further evidence of Veronese ability to intercept enemy messengers.

The Paduans kept their distance from the *bastida* of the Castagnaro, crossing the canal at an unknown point to the south of the stronghold trough a passage in the swamp. Once Castelbaldo came in sight, as foreseen by the Veronese leadership, all hell broke loose within the Paduan ranks, discipline and order collapsing while soldiers tried to outrun each other in a race to see who reached the supplies first. Hawkwood and Ubaldini urged Francesco Novello to restore order, but the younger Carrara could do nothing to stem the tide of running soldiers. Ubaldini and Sir John's own commands appear not to have been contaminated by the madness afflicting the rest of the army. They pitched camp on the right side of the Adige and behind the ditch that the Veronese had used when trying to stop Hawkwood and the younger Carrara a month before. There these experienced and disciplined troops spent the night of 10–11 March in miserable conditions while their comrades revelled inside Castelbaldo.

At sunrise a messenger arrived bearing the fateful news that the Veronese were approaching. Immediately, Francesco Novello took to the saddle and galloped to Castelbaldo in an attempt to rally his troops, but once in town he received the unpleasant surprise of discovering that ten days' worth of victuals had nearly all disappeared. Somehow, he managed to salvage the remaining supplies and send them to the camp across the Adige. He was much less successful in convincing his men to march out of the walls, even by threatening them with execution and by promising monetary benefits. As he returned to his headquarters across the river the despondent Francesco Novello bumped into Guglielmo Curtarolo, one of his father's most trusted officials as well as a skilled diplomat, who informed him that the Veronese, 'four times more than the Paduans', were approaching fast and recommended he retreat to safety. Carrara dismissed the idea out of hand, asking Cultarolo instead to go to Castelbaldo and try to convince the soldiers to return to their posts.

Cultarolo had evidently more convincing arguments than Francesco Novello's, since the Paduan troops started trickling back to the camp. It is quite possible that Curtarolo assured these men that Francesco il Vecchio would provide the same thing his son had already promised but could not deliver: more money. While we may consider this akin to extortion on the soldiers' part, they also had reasons to blame their employers, Francesco Novello in particular, for all the hardship they had suffered in the last three weeks, seeing it as a breach of contract. In the end, and despite all these efforts and promises, only about half the Paduan troops returned to their battle stations, the rest preferring the safety of Castelbaldo's walls and the supplies within.

Once the younger Carrara arrived at the camp he called a war council to determine the best course of action. The general mood was sullen, and nobody seemed to have a clear idea what to do. Hawkwood, Ubaldini and Biancardo took Francesco Novello aside and asked about his intentions: 'I'll answer after hearing your advice', came the reply. In the end, everyone wanted to defer to Hawkwood. Cornered, the English captain expressed the idea that a battle was the only option, adding however that Francesco Novello should ride off to safety 'for should the unfortunate occurrence happen of we losing and you being captured, your regime will be at risk'. Ubaldini endorsed Hawkwood's opinion, 'since should we be defeated, which shall not happen, we can find one-thousand remedies for such a fate, but you none'. Ugolotto Biancardo, however, proceeded to gut this sound advice by stating: 'I've never run from peasants, and he who will try to stop me is a brave man indeed'. Then Carrara blurted that he was no coward and intended to stay and fight.

There was more than one reason for Hawkwood and Ubaldini to want Francesco out of the way. Apart from their overt political motivations, they knew that his presence would be a magnet for the enemy, with the risk of the Paduan line where he was stationed collapsing under a number of attackers. Besides, Novello's handling of the campaign until then had caused Hawkwood and the other commanders to question his military abilities; and, although technically in command, Sir John could do little to countermand the son of the lord of Padua's wishes, even if they should result in tactical blunders. Honour and reputation also demanded that while Francesco Novello remained in the field, a possible retreat to Castelbaldo was out of the question.

Even if forced to fight in unfavourable circumstances, Hawkwood calculated he could make the best of a bad situation. He had already started to formulate a battle plan – although a risky one to implement, depending as it did on resistance, timing and getting the enemy into the right position. For the latter two, Sir John could count on his own ability and his troops' prowess. As for the resistance, he could only hope the Paduans would endure the enemy onslaught long enough without breaking.

Once the meeting ended, Hawkwood asked Ubaldini to form a battle array, but his co-commander excused himself by deferring to Sir John's superior experience. As the Paduans prepared themselves for battle – Cermisone's infantry setting the example – the English captain insisted that the troops should first eat and drink, knowing full well the devastating effects of a gruelling fight on an empty stomach. Francesco Novello had other plans. Leaving his commanders to deal with the more mundane aspects of battlefield organization, he retired to his living quarters, intending to enjoy what he reckoned to be a well-deserved breakfast.

THE BATTLE

THE APPROACH

Padua

We can imagine Francesco Novello nearly choking on his food when Giovanni d'Azzo degli Ubaldini burst into his quarters, 'completely armed, with his head covered by a pearl-studded hat and holding the baton of command', blurting: 'My lord Francesco, is this the time to eat? The enemy is nigh: get on your horse!' Ubaldini had set the spurs into his charger on noticing Carrara's absence from the battle line. A sheepish Francesco Novello, who – to his credit – had already donned armour, put on a jupon with the Carrara arms and a bascinet with his personal crest, before riding on his charger across the now-repaired pontoon bridge to join the army.

Hawkwood had deployed his troops with care on a front of about one kilometre in length, keeping in mind the strengths and weaknesses of each unit. On the far left flank stood Bartolomeo Cermisone with his *provvisionati* infantry: 800 spearmen, 400 crossbowmen and an unspecified number of pavisiers. Tough and resilient, these veteran foot-soldiers were also the most

The levee against which John Hawkwood anchored his right flank at the beginning of the battle of Castagnaro. He stationed several of his longbowmen on top of the levee to shoot at the Veronese left flank. (Author's Collection)

distant from Castelbaldo and therefore less likely to make a dash for the river should the going get too hot. The main body, nominally under Francesco Novello da Carrara, but in reality led by Ugolotto Biancardo, had a strength of 1,400 dismounted horsemen deployed in multiple ranks. Given their placement and Carrara's presence it was to be expected that these troops would take the brunt of the fight and therefore relied on strength in numbers. The right flank was taken up by Ubaldini and his 1,000 dismounted cavalry, possibly the best contingent in the Paduan army, except for Hawkwood's. Sir John's own command of 500 men-at-arms and 500 archers was stationed at the extreme right near the levee on the Adige, on top of which Cermisone had placed a group of infantry to strengthen the position. Seeing this, Ugolotto Biancardo pointed out that these men would be in peril should the Veronese launch an amphibious attack from the Adige 'and Sir Francesco and his captains being made aware of the matter they recognized such fears to be grounded, therefore correcting the situation'.

The last phrase is somewhat cryptic and neither Galeazzo nor Andrea Gatari see fit to add any clarifying information. How was the situation corrected? We know that these infantrymen were not recalled, since they remained on the levee until after the initial clash, and we have no news of other troops sent to reinforce them. One possible explanation, which actually fits with the battle dynamics, is that Hawkwood placed his longbowmen on a line of roughly 50m from the beginning of the levee's slope to its top, slightly behind the English men-at-arms and Cermisone's men. This allowed those archers not only to have a good range of shot but also to intercept any troops – presumably from the *bastida* of Castagnaro – attempting to execute an outflanking manoeuvre by boat. While fully equipped men-at-arms were largely impervious to arrows – except when shot at point-blank range and by a very skilled archer – infantrymen, on the other hand, often had many exposed parts of the body, usually the legs, the arms or the face. Therefore, foot-soldiers trying to disembark below the levee on the side of the Adige would have been shot to pieces by Hawkwood's bowmen even before they reached the foot of the slope.

Sir John had chosen his position well; in fact, he was helped in this by Della Scala himself. As already mentioned, the lord of Verona had ordered the digging of a ditch as an advanced defence for the *bastida* at the Castagnaro, possibly enlarging an already extant drainage canal running for about one kilometre from the levee to the swamp. Now it was employed as a defence by the Paduans: the ditch was some 4m wide and with deep, sloping banks, an unsurpassable obstacle for cavalry and a formidable one for soldiers on foot. Hawkwood had ordered that about 10m of the ditch facing his position be filled in, enough to allow a body of men to move forward across it without excessively impairing its defensive value. Still, he worried that this little piece of flat land could prove rather too tempting for an attacking enemy. Therefore, he wanted to make sure that the Veronese attention be diverted from the filled-in portion of the ditch. The English archers on the slopes of the levee would make sure of that.

The battlefield layout favoured the defenders. We know from contemporary sources that the valley 'narrowed' towards the ditch, something not immediately apparent today. Although the Adige now runs straight, in 1387 its course was characterized by numerous bends. One of these intruded forcefully onto the battlefield, and where once was the peak

of its curve, a ditch of the appropriate length can still be seen, although we cannot be absolutely sure if it was the one used by the Paduans. The Adige's bend, combined with the swamp created by the now filled-in Castagnaro canal, would have given the impression of a confined space, in fact one designed, although unwittingly, to funnel the attacking Veronese and deny them the advantage of full deployment. When Hawkwood had agreed to give battle, he had taken a calculated risk; but knowing full well that if he had to fight he could not have chosen a better defensive position.

With a large portion of the Paduan troops still in Castelbaldo, Hawkwood could not afford any reserves. At the rear of the formation stood approximately 200 horse, including some Paduan gentlemen, under Antonio Pio and Arcoano Buzzacarini, Francesco Novello's uncle, to whom Hawkwood also entrusted 'the great Carrara banner'. The translation of the phrase in Venetian-Paduan language '*Zuane Agudo de' la gienerale bandiera dal caro*', has been misinterpreted in the past to indicate the presence of the Paduan *carroccio* (war wagon), translating *dal* as 'from the' instead of the correct 'with the' – the Paduan banner displaying the Carrara arms of a red wagon on a white field. This said, Andrea Gatari does use the term *carroccio* in connection with this banner but, since his father, Galeazzo, never mentions the war wagon, Andrea is referring to the Carrara standard alone. In reality, the *carroccio*, once an important feature in the armies of Italy's city-states, had long since disappeared from the battlefield.

Verona

Hawkwood had barely finished deploying his men than the Veronese army came in sight. As Della Scala's troops drew nearer, the Paduans were dismayed

Although it has diminished significantly since 1387, the width of the original ditch on the battlefield of Castagnaro behind which Hawkwood positioned his troops can still be seen from the levee in the green grass outline. The portion filled in by Hawkwood lies between the tree (a later growth) and levee. (Author's Collection)

to see 'so many people that one could hardly believe it be true, causing all our men to hesitate'. Once again, Sir John and the other commanders urged Francesco Novello to seek safety inside Castelbaldo, only to receive a firm refusal. Instead, to encourage any soldiers whose resolve might be wavering, he knighted four of his kinsmen and Bernardo degli Scolari on the field; Hawkwood and Ubaldini personally bestowed spurs on the new *cavalieri*. Sir John then dubbed as knights 'many foreigners as a sign of victory'. This show of confidence over, the Paduans waited anxiously for the oncoming clash. Hawkwood prudently had all the horses sent well to the rear, to avoid the risk of people deserting in the heat of battle.

Giovanni degli Ordelaffi, the official commander of Della Scala's host, probably knew already what to expect, scouts from the *bastida* of the Castagnaro being able to forward information about the enemy array, since we know that 'he constantly received news about the Carrara army'. The Veronese forces advanced ready for battle, divided into six major mounted units, with the infantry and the artillery trailing behind. Once Ordelaffi caught sight of the Paduans' deployment he rode back and commanded Giovanni dell'Ischia, in charge of the Veronese foot, to organize his men for the battle. Ischia arrayed the Veronese on a slightly elevated meadow surrounded by canals near the Adige. It was a large mass of men, even if we dismiss Andrea Gatari's estimate of 2,600 professional infantry and 16,000 country levies as exaggerations. More prosaically, Galeazzo Gatari states that between 'citizens of Verona and peasants' there were more than six times in number 'those of Padua'. It is unclear if Gatari is referring to the Paduan infantry under Cermisone or to those auxiliaries present in every army of the time. Still, if we take as a yardstick the already-mentioned Veronese administrative document of the previous year, 6,000–7,000 infantry between paid and militia appears a fair estimate.

Ordelaffi was joined by Ostasio da Polenta in giving instructions to the soldiers manning the multi-barrelled artillery pieces. What these orders may have been we can only guess – Galeazzo Gatari gives us no

Looking down the ditch from the base of the levee, the 1387 width is clear from the greener grass. It is more difficult to imagine the depth. The original sources describe it as able to be crossed; however, the troops had to make both a steep descent and assent to do so. (Author's Collection)

further information and Andrea Gatari fails entirely to mention these guns before the battle. However, from the evidence at hand we can presume that Ordelaffi and Polenta's directions referred to the designated position of the gun carts within the Veronese formation and their distance from the enemy. Next, the Veronese leaders prepared for battle, as the cavalry units took up their designated position in the field at the shout of 'Scala, Scala! Carne, carne!' (Scala, Scala! Flesh, flesh!), to which the Paduans responded with 'Carne, carne!' The latter has been interpreted as a ferocious variation of the cry 'Carro, Carro!' normally used by Carrara's soldiers; in fact, carne was quite a widespread battle cry, indicating a determination to fight to the finish – at least within the brackets of standard Italian military practice.

Ordelaffi's 1,000 horse under his deputy Ugolino dal Verme took up the left of the line, in front of Hawkwood's contingent. The Count d'Ancre placed his 800 cavalry facing Ubaldini, against whom, apparently, he nursed a personal grudge. Ostasio da Polenta took the centre at the head of 1,000 mounted troops, next to Benedetto da Malcesine with 800. Finally, the Veronese right, flanking the swamp, was held by Taddeo dal Verme with 600 horse. At the rear stood the Veronese banners, guarded by 1,000 cavalry that included 'many gentlemen from Verona' and described as the 'most select brigade ever'. These were under the command of the *condottiere* and man of letters Ludovico Cantelli. Seeing the Paduan defensive position, Ordelaffi ordered his men to dismount, except for Cantelli's unit, as the Veronese commander awaited the arrival of the artillery carts.

The numbers of both armies come from Galeazzo Gatari, giving a total of 3,100 dismounted horsemen and 1,900+ infantry (including archers) for the Paduans, versus 5,200 dismounted cavalry for the Veronese. Still, these rough equivalents hide the true Veronese advantage. Apart from the technological edge given by the artillery, Della Scala's commanders could also count on thousands of infantrymen waiting in the rear to join the fray. Although described by the elder Gatari as 'rabble', nevertheless the sheer size of Verona's foot could prove a determining factor against the numerically inferior Paduans. By choosing to fight in a restricted place, Hawkwood had done much to negate this particular advantage; indeed, all evidence points to the fact that Ordelaffi simply did not have enough space to deploy all his troops.

The question of both armies' strength is complicated by the breakdown given by Andrea Gatari.

***Cavalli* and cavalry units at Castagnaro**

	Verona: Mounted divisions	Verona: Horses	Padua: Mounted divisions	Padua: Horses
Galeazzo Gatari	6	5,200	3	3,100
Andrea Gatari	12	9,400	8	6,900

We may ascribe such a discrepancy to Andrea's desire to magnify Padua's victory following a pattern acquired – by his own admission – from Livy and Virgil. The elder Gatari's take is further confirmed by a Florentine diplomatic document written a few days after the battle, stating that 'more than 3,000 lances were involved'. If we take the standard three-man lance as a basis, the total number comes to at least 9,000 cavalry – pretty close to the total

From here the Castagnaro battlefield towards the Veronese left flank from Hawkwood's right flank can be seen. (Author's Collection)

of Galeazzo Gatari, who also adds that the Veronese army numbered more than 14,000 men; which makes sense, if one includes auxiliaries, together with sappers and miners.

Once he had arrayed his army, Giovanni degli Ordelaffi is reputed to have delivered a speech to the troops, encouraging everyone to do the utmost in taking the ditch, emphasizing the glory to be gained with victory and the money to be made with ransoms 'for the greater part of Padua's army was made up of its richest citizens'; besides, the enemy was inferior in numbers, tired and hungry. Thus he urged, in the name of Saint George (Verona's patron saint) and the lord Antonio Della Scala, every effort should be made to obtain victory. Francesco Novello, on the other hand, used a rather more

From the levee next to the battlefield the original placement of the Veronese left flank and centre can be seen (approximately at the location of the green growth in the distance). As the Veronese approached, longbow shot from Hawkwood's archers would cause the troops to angle away from the levee toward the centre of the Paduan line. (Author's Collection)

down-to-earth form of encouragement by promising double pay and a 'full month' of wages. Only Andrea Gatari records these facts, but they ring true in the light of other available evidence.

The armies were now ready, probably no more than 150m apart. The commanders and men on both sides eagerly and anxiously readied the opening shots – literally as the Veronese awaited their gunpowder artillery to be in position. Instead, Hawkwood needed to get Della Scala's troops moving before their arrival. One contemporary, if unreliable, Florentine chronicle erroneously states that Sir John sent forward the Paduan *saccomanni* (mounted foragers) to goad his adversaries into action. Hawkwood did not need mounted cavalrymen: he already had a far more effective system to obtain his purpose, one tested successfully time and time again on the battlefields of Western Europe for more than 50 years.

'LIKE FIRE-SPITTING DRAGONS'

It was around 3.30 in the afternoon of 11 March 1387, 'when the sun was rapidly travelling towards the dampened earth', that it started to rain. Yet these particular drops were not intended to further soak the field already damp and muddy from the previous days' showers. Ordelaffi's soldiers started being hit by English arrows. Hawkwood's decision to have his archers shoot in the midst of Della Scala's left flank is implied by Galeazzo Gatari and openly stated by other, later, authors. It does, however, make sense. Sir John needed the Veronese to advance before the arrival of their artillery, counting, correctly, on the galling effect a flurry of projectiles could deliver. We should not, however, imagine the longbowmen shooting an uninterrupted barrage of arrows; and certainly not the 50,000 arrows in one minute, as calculated by one recent author. Rather, as made clear from contemporary accounts of other battles, Hawkwood's archers would have released three volleys in sequence before pausing to recuperate from the physical exertion of drawing a bow and being careful not to empty their quivers. Yet, their action proved no less unnerving than one of continuous shooting so beloved by film directors and armchair historians.

Most of the arrows probably bounced off the metal protections worn by Ordelaffi's men-at-arms, but occasionally a pointed shaft would find its way into a joint in the armour or hit an exposed part of the body: the face if the visor was up; or the limbs of those less well-equipped soldiers. As screams of pain started being heard, the Veronese instinctively stepped forward, in an attempt to avoid the incoming sharpened points. Whether or not the Veronese interpreted this as a sign to attack, they started moving as one body towards the enemy. Though, Gatari suggests, this attack was not made in full against Hawkwood's troops, but against where they joined Ubaldini's force. The English arrows seem to have pushed Ordelaffi's men to take this somewhat diagonal course, we can surmise, because they were holding their shields high as an extra safeguard against the flying shafts and could not advance straight forward.

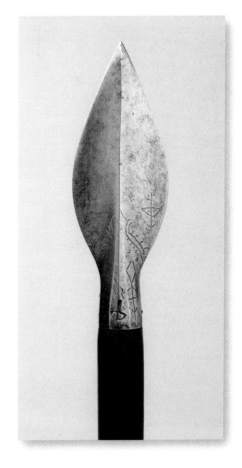

Lanceheads of all lengths and sizes have been found in Europe dating to the Middle Ages. Because of this, and the uncertainty of contemporary artistic depictions, we cannot determine which were used for combat, rather than hunting or jousting. The Metropolitan Museum of Art places this lancehead in Italy during the later 14th century. (The Metropolitan Museum of Art, New York)

PADUAN FORCES

A. 200 infantry and 500 English archers on the levee near the Adige.

B. Sir John Hawkwood and 500 English men-at-arms.

C. Giovanni degli Ubaldini and 1,000 cavalry.

D. Francesco Novello da Carrara and 1,400 cavalry.

E. Cermisone da Parma with 800 infantry, 400 crossbowmen and a number of pavisiers.

F. Reserve, 200 cavalry under Antonio Pio.

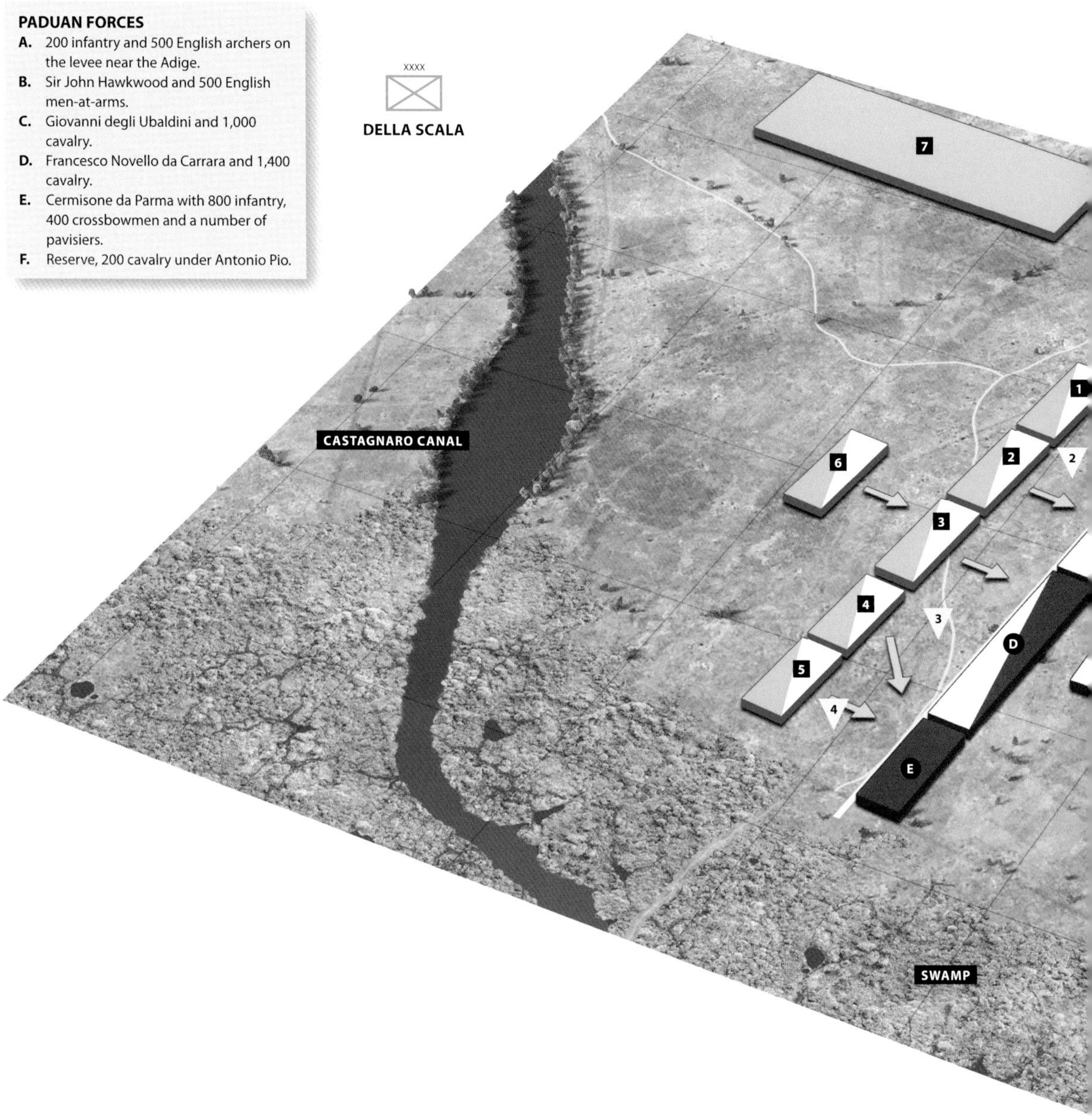

xxxx

DELLA SCALA

CASTAGNARO CANAL

SWAMP

EVENTS

1. Hawkwood's archers start shooting against the Veronese left flank.

2. Galled by the volleys, the Veronese start moving forward, the left flank at an angle in the direction of Ubaldini's contingent. Thus, Hawkwood's command is not fully engaged.

3. The Veronese centre hits the Paduan main battle focusing its effort against Francesco da Carrara's position.

4. The Paduan infantry is engaged by the Veronese left flank; it is reinforced by the Veronese reserve, leaving a small contingent to guard the Della Scala banners.

5. The 200 or-so Paduan infantry with Hawkwood's archers are ordered to reinforce Ubaldini's troops.

VERONESE FORCES
1. Giovanni degli Ordelaffi and 1,000 cavalry.
2. The Count d'Ancre and 800 cavalry.
3. Ostasio da Polenta and 1,000 cavalry.
4. Benedetto da Malcesine and 800 cavalry.
5. Taddeo dal Verme and 600 cavalry.
6. Reserve, 1,000 cavalry under Lodovico Cantelli.
7. Infantry, 6,000–7,000 mostly militia under Giovanni dell'Ischia.

ADIGE RIVER

PONTOON BRIDGE

CASTELBALDO

NOVELLO

THE OPENING PHASE, 3:30–4:00PM

Spurred by the arrow barrage of Hawkwood's bowmen,
the Veronese hit the Paduan line.

Given the sodden ground and the need to keep formation, it may have taken the Veronese up to three minutes to cover the distance separating them from the Paduan-held ditch, their pace undoubtedly increasing as they neared their objective. Both sides lowered their long cavalry lances, the Veronese trusting in their momentum to carry the ditch and break the Paduan line. The blast of opposing trumpets mixed with the din of lance-heads hitting armour created a cacophony only increased by the respective battle shouts, the cries of '*Scala*' and '*Carne*' filling the afternoon air. But the combination of the ditch and Paduan weapons blunted the Veronese onslaught, the defenders holding fast as they struggled to retain their footing in a match resembling what decades later would be known as 'push of pike'.

Because of its slanted approach, only part of Ordelaffi's unit came into contact with Sir John's contingent, the rest joining with Ancre's soldiers against Ubaldini's troops. Soon Ubaldini found himself hard pressed, despite his men's resilience and his own personal display of valour. Seeing this, Ugolotto Biancardo ordered the infantry on the levee to reinforce Ubaldini, the threat from the river not having materialized. Hawkwood's archers were presumably still shooting at Ordelaffi's men-at-arms, thus keeping them from turning their full attention to their front, especially where the ditch had been filled in. Although Hawkwood had consciously put Ubaldini in peril, he trusted his colleague to resist the more numerous Veronese facing him; and Ubaldini would show himself worthy of Sir John's trust.

The fiercest fighting was happening in the centre, Carrara's presence attracting the Veronese like flies to honey. Facing Francesco Novello's men-at-arms were the combined forces of Ostasio da Polenta and Benedetto da Malcesine, their lances going for the conspicuous target of the son of Padua's

The battlefield of Castagnaro from the levee. The first green line indicates the ditch behind which the Padua army was positioned at the beginning of the battle. The Veronese right flank and centre moved to engage the army there – near the silo in the distance to the right – where the main part of the battle was fought. (Author's Collection)

Come mess Ghirardo dappiano corse pisa plu

o pertucto pisa gridando uiua mess Gerard dappiano

ruling lord. Francesco Novello nearly went to the ground under the force of the many lance thrusts directed at him, only the packed human wall of the nearby men keeping him on his feet. Never one to shy away from a brawl, Carrara and Biancardo at his side are described akin to 'fire-spitting dragons' as they attempted to push back the Veronese assault. Brave to the point of recklessness, Francesco put the cohesion of the Paduan line and the battle's outcome in jeopardy when he tried to cross the ditch to get closer to the enemy. For his pain he received in return many blows, 'like a hammer in a forge'. Several of those who tried to follow him fell into the ditch and there his cousin, Francesco Buzzacarino, was severely wounded. As a testimony to the civility of Italian warfare, a local truce was called to allow the retrieval of the unfortunate Buzzacarino.

Despite such shows of courtesy, blood was being spilt in abundance as the number of dead and, even more, wounded piled up on both sides. Determined to avenge his kinsman, a furious Francesco Novello delivered a massive lance thrust against Ostasio da Polenta, throwing him down; however, the Veronese leader was immediately picked up by his men, returning to the fray unscathed – evidence of the quality of his armour. That good bodily protection went a long way to protect its wearer was confirmed a few seconds later when one of Polenta's household struck Carrara in the side with a boar-spear (*ghiavarina*), 'piercing his jupon, armour, mail and even reaching the flesh where it left a large bruise; but, thank God, it did no other damage'. Francesco continued fighting, seemingly unfazed by the incident.

On the Paduan left, Cermisone's infantry faced Taddeo dal Verme and Ludovico Cantelli, the latter evidently sent as a reinforcement, since the Paduan foot outnumbered Taddeo's contingent two to one. If the Veronese leaders believed that this would produce a breakthrough then they

Another illumination from Sercambi's *Le croniche di Lucca* depicts units of cavalry riding through town. Leading the second unit is a trumpeter and standard carrier holding the banners of the unit while three soldiers raise swords rather than lances (another does the same at the rear of the preceding unit). This probably denotes their leadership, although the captain of the rear unit is clearly the lone horseman wearing armour, with a cap rather than a helmet, and carrying what likely was a baton of office. (Archivio di Stato di Lucca, f. 279v. Authorisation 87/19. Su concessione del Ministero dei Beni e delle Attività Culturali e del Turismo. Duplicazione e riproduzione vietata con qualsiasi mezzo)

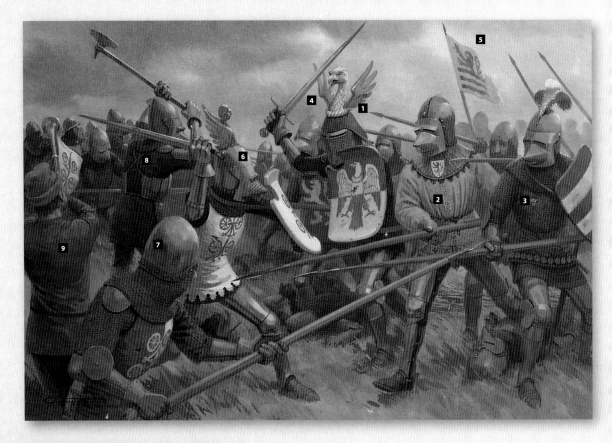

THE VERONESE BREAKTHROUGH (PP. 68–69)

As the Veronese carry the ditch, the Paduan line starts to crack in the face of superior numbers. The scene depicts this dramatic moment of the battle. Ostasio da Polenta (1), leads the Veronese assault, the crested great-helm he wears over a bascinet a visible rallying point for his men. At his left are the German knight Georg von Schönberg (2) and the Veronese Ugolino dal Verme (3). Schönberg is clad in a Mittle-European coat with long, loose sleeves and wears a bascinet with a klappvisor, somewhat demodée in Italy but still popular north of the Alps. Dal Verme's armour is a combination of up-to-date and earlier pieces, his family's fortune taking-off once again after years of exile from Verona. Coming up behind Polenta is the feudal lord Antonio da Castelbarco (4) leading a group of his own retainers, the latter's mixture of older and newer equipment denoting different degrees of individual wealth. The banner of Giovanni degli Ordelaffi (5) indicates that the Veronese left flank has by now moved towards the centre of the line, adding weight to the attempted breakthrough.

On the Paduan side, Francesco Novello da Carrara (6) desperately tries to stem the mounting Veronese tide. As would be expected from a member of one of the most powerful Italian families, his apparel is the best on the market. From contemporary sources we know he wore a crested bascinet rather than Polenta's great helm, but carries the same *bouche* style of shield, a shape that was becoming increasingly popular in Italy. At Francesco Novello's side a member of his household (7) moves in to protect his lord, his role and position evident from the variant of the Carrara arms on his jupon. Also guarding Francesco Novello, this anonymous Paduan man-at-arms (8), whose state-of-the-art breastplate has caused him to forgo his jupon, although one could expect him to have some sort of field sign painted on his armour for the sake of recognition. The Paduan trumpeter (9) sports the Carrara arms on the small flag hanging from his instrument, but otherwise wears normal civilian clothes.

miscalculated badly, for the Paduan foot put up a spirited fight against the more heavily armoured opponents. Besides, throwing Cantelli's men-at-arms into the fray meant that the Della Scala banners were left with very little protection, a situation resembling that of the Brentelle. However, the Veronese were sufficiently confident of their success to run such a risk.

Hawkwood had been watching the battle on the right and now decided to see for himself how matters were going in the rest of the field. Leaving Giovanni Tarlati da Pietramala in command of his contingent, Sir John mounted his horse and rode towards the centre. Seeing Francesco Novello hard pressed by the enemy, he managed to get him out of the line and strongly suggested he remove himself with his household troops to the right flank, where the fighting, evidently, was less intense – this giving substance to the argument that the English contingent was not then fully engaged. Francesco appeared to agree, only to throw himself once more into the struggle. Noticing this, the freshly knighted Bernardo degli Scolari shouted to those Paduan leaders nearer to Carrara: 'Gentlemen captains, force my lord Francesco da Carrara to mount his horse and leave the battle!' only to receive from Francesco the curt answer that he intended to stay until the fight had ended.

In another detail from the Frits Lugt drawing, soldiers fight in battle. Their chaotic conflict shows little organization and training, simply soldiers whacking away at each other. Those carrying shields use swords single-handedly, while those without wield hammers, mallets and swords with both hands. The results of these blows can be seen in the number of soldiers who have fallen. (Fondation Custodia, Collection Frits Lugt, Paris)

Carrara's obstinate stance was putting the battle's outcome at risk for the Paduans, since it had become clear that the primary objective of the Veronese was now to kill or capture the son of Padua's ruling lord. Again, Hawkwood, this time accompanied by Ubaldini and other Paduan leaders, begged Francesco to seek the safety of Castelbaldo; once again he retorted furiously that he would not leave, even if it should result in his death. Hearing the answer, Sir John threw away his baton and shouted, 'everyone return to battle!' He, sword in hand and shouting '*carne, carne*!' joined the fighting on the right flank where the ditch had been filled in. Sir John's theatrical gesture of discarding his symbol of command has been interpreted in various ways. But Galeazzo Gatari makes it clear that the English captain's gesture was born out of frustration in the face of Francesco Novello's rash stubbornness and not as a way to incite his men to perform some heroic deed.

The Veronese pulled back and regrouped, Ordelaffi, surveying the battle from the saddle, now ordering a general push against the Paduan centre. Trumpets sounded and Della Scala's troops tried again to cross the ditch, according to Andrea Gatari by filling it with fascines – not impossible, since they would have been readily available from the siege train at the

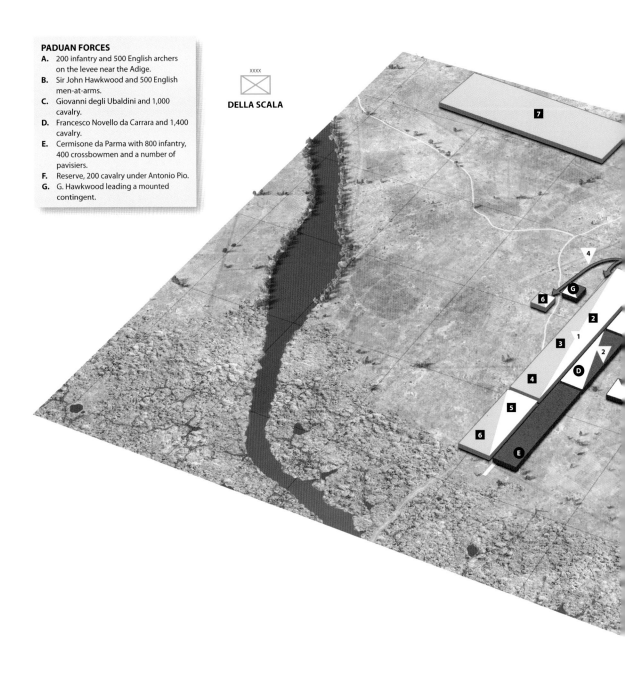

PADUAN FORCES

A. 200 infantry and 500 English archers on the levee near the Adige.

B. Sir John Hawkwood and 500 English men-at-arms.

C. Giovanni degli Ubaldini and 1,000 cavalry.

D. Francesco Novello da Carrara and 1,400 cavalry.

E. Cermisone da Parma with 800 infantry, 400 crossbowmen and a number of pavisiers.

F. Reserve, 200 cavalry under Antonio Pio.

G. G. Hawkwood leading a mounted contingent.

XXXX

DELLA SCALA

EVENTS

1. After an hour of fighting, the Veronese left and main battle concentrate their efforts on breaking the centre of the Paduan line, gaining a foothold on the other side of the ditch, after filling it with fascines, thus freeing Hawkwood's troops.

2. The Paduan line starts to waver, as Ubaldini's contingent and the main battle start feeling the increasing pressure, compounded by Francesco Novello da Carrara's refusal to abandon the field.

3. Seeing his chance, Hawkwood leads a body of men-at-arms and the Paduan infantry previously sent to reinforce Ubaldini on the opposite side of the ditch, crossing it at the point where it had previously been filled-in. Under the covering volleys of their archers, the 'English' hit the flank and rear of the Veronese left.

4. Hawkwood leads a small mounted contingent against the Veronese banners, unhorsing Francesco Visconti and snatching from him the great Della Scala standard.

VERONESE FORCES
1. Giovanni degli Ordelaffi and 1,000 cavalry.
2. The Count d'Ancre and 800 cavalry.
3. Ostasio da Polenta and 1,000 cavalry.
4. Benedetto da Malcesine and 800 cavalry.
5. Taddeo dal Verme and Lodovico Cantelli with 1,600 cavalry.
6. Veronese banners, guarded by a small contingent under Francesco Visconti.
7. Infantry, 6,000–7,000 mostly militia under Giovanni dell'Ischia.

xxxx

NOVELLO

THE CRISIS, 4:00–5:20PM

As the Veronese push the Paduans to a near-breaking point, they leave their flank and rear dangerously exposed.

Approximately where the trees end in the centre of the photograph is where John Hawkwood saw the Veronese banners, unprotected in the chaos of battle except by a small number of men. Riding with his retinue diagonally from his position at the end of the right Paduan flank, he surprised the Veronese guard and captured their standards. (Author's Collection)

Veronese army's rear. Galeazzo Gatari simplifies matters by stating that sheer weight of numbers allowed some of Della Scala's men to climb the banks and drive home their assault. As the Veronese gained a foothold on the opposite side of the ditch, the Carrara men-at-arms abandoned their lances for swords and axes, and, in a determined counter-attack, managed to push back the enemy troops. Each and all the Paduan units were now engaged in a desperate hand-to-hand struggle, 'the ground turning crimson from the blood flowing abundantly from the cruel wounds'. Each and all... except for Hawkwood's.

'A MOST PROFICIENT LEADER IN MILITARY AFFAIRS'

From his position on the right flank, Sir John was watching apprehensively as the battle at the centre swung to and fro, becoming clearer by the minute that it would be only a matter of time before the Paduan line collapsed. Hawkwood noticed the Della Scala banner standing virtually unprotected behind the enemy and seized the chance. Via messenger, Sir John informed Ubaldini that he intended to rush the Veronese standard, adding 'and you then decide what to do in accordance with the action's outcome'. Far from being the result of a carefully laid-out plan, as Hawkwood's fans would have us believe, his was a decision born out of desperation, with the rationale that at this point he had little to lose in taking the initiative. However, Sir John, 'a most proficient leader in military affairs', to quote Galeazzo Gatari, could count on the discipline and experience of his men-at-arms and archers. For the sake of some extra punch, he pulled out of the line those infantrymen previously sent to reinforce Ubaldini, even at the risk of aiding a Veronese breakthrough.

Hawkwood's men crossed the ditch under the cover of the archers' protective barrage. Most were probably on foot. Neither the elder nor the younger Gatari mentions horses, and the lack of time combined with the few metres of levelled ground would not have allowed for the deployment of cavalry – although judging the action's dynamics, it is possible that Sir John and a few of his officers were mounted.

Once a sufficient number of men had passed the filled-in portion of the ditch, Hawkwood issued a straightforward order: hit the enemy hard in the flank and rear, Della Scala's banners the primary objective. Sir John's timing could not have been better. By now the Veronese had gained a permanent foothold on the other side of the ditch, slowly but surely pushing back the Paduan defenders. Francesco Novello, in the thick of the fight, had risked on several occasions being captured, every time saved by the concerted efforts of his immediate followers. Believing victory firmly in his grasp, Ordelaffi sent orders to Giovanni dell'Ischia that he bring forward the Veronese infantry to finish the Paduans for good.

Charging diagonally across the field, Hawkwood's men struck the flank and the rear of the Veronese left with the force of a mallet. Fully absorbed by the fighting in front of them, Della Scala's soldiers did not realize what had hit them until too late. As the English dismounted horse and the Paduan foot proceeded to roll up the Veronese left, Hawkwood with a few followers went straight for the enemy flags, pulling from his horse Francesco Visconti, entrusted with Della Scala's great banner, and casting the Veronese standard into the mud. Hearing the noise behind them, Ordelaffi and da Polenta turned around to see their insignia down and, worse still, their retreat blocked by Hawkwood's soldiers. Word of what had happened spread like wildfire down the length of the Veronese line, the cohesion of Della Scala's units at first fraying and then starting to split at the seams, the men's fighting spirit faltering.

Freed from enemy pressure, the Paduans crossed the ditch cleaving their way through the enemy ranks with little opposition. Francesco Novello and Biancardo mounted their chargers and rode to Hawkwood's position, a quick look at the battlefield enough to assess the situation. Hammered between Sir John's men and the Paduans, the Veronese were being pressed against the impassable swamp to the south; many had already attempted to get to their horses, the cramped space slowing and impeding their movements. Those Veronese lucky enough to reach their mounts rode off the field with all speed; the majority, however, had no time before finding themselves overwhelmed by superior numbers and forced to surrender in droves.

Reduced to a force of about 200 men-at-arms, Ordelaffi and Polenta were forced to surrender to Francesco Novello in person, as the Paduans, having recovered their own mounts, gave chase to the defeated Veronese. In the ensuing confusion, somehow the Count d'Ancre,

From the east of where the battle was fought (roughly where the present ditch ends), the tilled field in the foreground gives us more-or-less the position of the Veronese banners with the levee in the background. (Author's Collection)

HAWKWOOD TURNS THE TIDE (PP. 76–77)

As the bulk of his contingent hits the flank of the Veronese left, Sir John Hawkwood leads a small mounted unit against the Della Scala banners. Here we see Sir John (1) pulling from the saddle the Veronese standard-bearer Francesco Visconti (2). Even if contemporary sources do not mention Hawkwood specifically as the one grappling Visconti, this is entirely possible: although in his mid-60s, Sir John was still a vigorous and active fighter, who led by example. Here he is shown wearing a full set of expensive cutting-edge Milanese armour, as befitted a *condottiere* of his calibre. In a desperate attempt to remain in the saddle, Visconti, wearing a crested great helm for immediate recognition, is about to drop the Della Scala great banner, the fall of which will trigger chaos among the Veronese. Coming up in Hawkwood's support is John Coe (3), one of Sir John's captains. He wears a very good

suit of armour, even if his command of 20 lances does not allow him to afford the very latest model. In contrast, Hawkwood's standard-bearer (4) is sporting a state-of-the-art breastplate, Sir John evidently keen that his own banner not hit the ground. The English man-at-arms assisting Hawkwood (5) is evidently a newcomer to Italy, his armour, as shown by the great-helm and the style of the cuisses, definitely foreign and old-fashioned by Italian standards. Should he reap enough booty on the field, this *inghilese* can hope to spruce himself up by the start of the next campaign. Completely surprised by Hawkwood's attack, the Veronese Ottaviano della Branca (6), makes a belated attempt to face the assailants – having lost the Della Scala banner at the battle of the Brentelle, the unfortunate Ottaviano is about to repeat this humiliating experience.

Benedetto da Malcesine and Ugolino dal Verme escaped the field at the head of about 800 cavalry. They managed to ride as far as Legnago, 16km to the north-east, before a pursuing force under Ubaldini, Biordo de' Michelotti – destined later to become the ruling lord of Perugia – Ceccolo Broglia – who would teach a whole generation of *condottieri* – and Filippo da Pisa caught up with them. Tired, battered and dispirited, the fugitives surrendered to their pursuers, being led back to the victors' camp.

The Veronese horse had been defeated but, before ending, the battle still had one more bloody chapter to write. Giovanni dell'Ischia had remained at his original position, events having made Ordelaffi's orders redundant. Now, at the head of a large, but makeshift and badly equipped infantry force he was about to face the full brunt of the victorious Paduans. Francesco Novello sent him a messenger requesting dell'Ischia's surrender, pointing out that since the rest of the Veronese army had been routed and captured any further resistance was futile and he should not let Christians die or be maimed just for pleasure. Dell'Ischia, however, was made of sterner stuff, replying that he preferred to fight to the death in the name of his lord's honour. Then Francesco himself took up the great Paduan standard and rode to where dell'Ischia's soldiers stood, with him Cermisone's infantry and those men-at-arms not allotted to guard the prisoners or busy chasing fugitives along the Adige. Thus, Francesco Novello's force must have been relatively small, although this would be a fight of quality against quantity.

This is likely the raised meadow where the Veronese militia stood. The immediate vicinity of the Adige River, here hidden on the right, made it a preferred escape route, although the river, broad and deep at this point, became a death-trap for many. (Author's Collection)

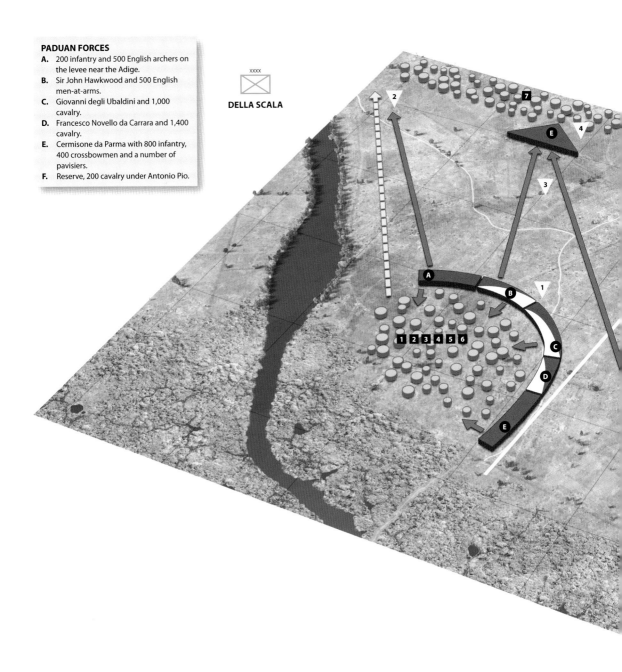

PADUAN FORCES

A. 200 infantry and 500 English archers on the levee near the Adige.

B. Sir John Hawkwood and 500 English men-at-arms.

C. Giovanni degli Ubaldini and 1,000 cavalry.

D. Francesco Novello da Carrara and 1,400 cavalry.

E. Cermisone da Parma with 800 infantry, 400 crossbowmen and a number of pavisiers.

F. Reserve, 200 cavalry under Antonio Pio.

xxxx

DELLA SCALA

EVENTS

1. Seeing their standard lost and pressed by Hawkwood's men, the Veronese start to waver and then break, the Paduans enveloping and pushing them towards the marsh to the south. The Veronese surrender in droves.

2. A large group of Veronese men-at-arms manages to take to the saddle and flee. They are followed by a mounted Paduan contingent and captured after a 10-mile chase.

3. Leaving a substantial force to guard the prisoners, the victorious Paduans march to the site where the Veronese militia is stationed. Calls to surrender are rebuffed by the Veronese commander Giovanni dell'Ischia.

4. Spearheaded by Cermisone da Parma's infantry, the Paduans attack in the waning light and slaughtering the poorly equipped Veronese, many of which drown in the Adige while trying to escape. Seeing the futility of further resistance, dell'Ischia, his honour saved, surrenders.

VERONESE FORCES

1. Giovanni degli Ordelaffi and 1,000 cavalry.
2. The Count d'Ancre and 800 cavalry.
3. Ostasio da Polenta and 1,000 cavalry.
4. Benedetto da Malcesine and 800 cavalry.
5. Taddeo dal Verme and 600 cavalry.
6. Reserve, 1,000 cavalry under Lodovico Cantelli.
7. Infantry, 6,000–7,000 mostly militia under Giovanni dell'Ischia.

xxxx

NOVELLO

THE SLAUGHTER, 5:20–6:15PM
The Veronese main army having disintegrated, Della Scala's militia is faced with a tough predicament.

LAST STAND ON THE ADIGE (PP. 82–83)

The final act of the battle of Castagnaro was a savage affair compared with the civility of the main encounter. In the dwindling daylight, a wary Francesco Novello da Carrara (1), banner in hand, his jupon slashed and cut, leads the assault against the Veronese foot, mostly ill-armed militiamen, orders being given by the sound of trumpets (2). In contrast with their opponents, the attacking Paduan infantry is made of professional *provvisionati*, as shown by their equipment: brigandines (3), padded jackets over mail (4), breastplates protecting the torso (5). Most wear open-faced bascinets or kettle-hats, although a few may have acquired visored helmets. Leg armour is significantly scarce, when in formation pavises and bucklers protecting the lower limbs; the exception is the junior officer (6) engaging an equivalent on the Veronese side. The crossbowman (7) has practically no armour except a bascinet and mail ventail; on the other hand, if behind a pavise he would not need any extra

protection, and when acting as a skirmisher would need all the speed possible to gain the safety of his ranks, should the going get tough. In the centre, one of Carrara's household members (8) – possibly the commander of the Paduan *provvisionati*, Cermisone da Parma – is engaging the Veronese infantry leader Giovanni dell'Ischia (9), the latter fully clad in armour, even if evidence exists of foot officers wearing *corazzine* (akin to brigandines, but with larger plates) rather than breastplates, for the sake of mobility. In the foreground, one of the many Veronese dead (10), militiamen mainly country folk and urban poor, with little more than a head piece and /or a few bits of armour for protection – if that. Near him a lead-headed mallet is visible, further evidence of the lack of fighting equipment among the Veronese foot. In the background, Veronese militiamen (11) attempt to climb the levee to flee the carnage, many of them meeting their end in the River Adige's muddy waters.

The Paduans attacked in the approaching dusk. The fight was short, ruthless and extremely bloody, the poorly armed militia no match for the hardened professionals. Francesco Novello, banner in hand, led the charge in person, with Cermisone's men following, cutting into the enemy formation like a hot knife through butter. Soon the air was filled with the screams of the wounded and the last gasps of the dying, broken lances littering and covering the fallen on the gory field. Closely packed together, the Veronese had no space to use their own weapons, while the dead still standing in the throng contributed to the impediment. Those fortunate enough not to be cut down immediately tried to surrender, called upon God and the saints for help, or attempted to flee towards the Adige. Many who made it to the river drowned in the murky waters. Seeing that all further resistance was useless, dell'Ischia accepted defeat, his men's blood having preserved his honour and reputation.

It was now about 6.00 in the afternoon, 'the sun's dark and humid halo descending to the dampened earth', after two hours of intense fighting the battle finally over. Returning to his quarters and exhausted but upbeat Francesco Novello immediately wrote to his father with the good news, adding to the missive his punctured, cut and slashed velvet jupon superimposed with the Carrara arms. One of the household servants was then dispatched to Padua on a good, fast horse. Francesco Novello would write for some time afterwards to communicate his victory to the towns of the Carrara domain, short notes with few details. In the one he sent to the Treviso municipality he mentioned only that the battle had been fought 'near the *bastida* of the Castagnaro (*prope bastitam Castagnari*), adding the names of the captured enemy leaders, Ordelaffi and da Polenta, plus 'all the other men of rank in the opposing army, together with their standards and banners'.

In another detail from the Frits Lugt drawing the aftermath of battle is seen. Soldiers are shown stripping the dead. Pieces of arm and elbow armour lay strewn where they have been thrown, next to a sword, spear, shield and helmet. This gruesome display followed every battle, with profit for those willing to loot the dead; among things taken, personal armour could be upgraded, with the rest sold on. (Fondation Custodia, Collection Frits Lugt, Paris)

Francesco did not bother to mention casualties but, the day after the battle, when the Venetian resident in Ferrara wrote to his government, he underscored the death of 'many peasants'. It is clear that the Veronese militia suffered the most, Galeazzo Gatari putting the number of the 'severely wounded' country folk at 846. He also adds that the total of Veronese killed 'on the blood-soaked field' came to 742, excluding therefore the many others drowned in the Adige. How many of Della Scala's men-at-arms were slain? It is impossible to give a correct answer, but if we take the number of fatalities suffered by the defeated side in other Italian land battles of the period we get a rough 5–7 per cent of the total force. Besides, if we subtract the number of fully equipped Veronese cavalry taken prisoners from the total of their original array we get a total of 580. Considering that some of the defeated army must have managed to get away, we can hypothesize that around 300–350 Veronese men-at-arms lost their lives at Castagnaro. No equivalent data exists for the Paduans, but we know that they suffered 'few wounded and even less killed'. Even allowing for a degree of exaggeration, it is clear that Carrara's casualties were much fewer than the enemy's.

Della Scala's army had ceased to exist as a fighting force, the worst losses being economic. The men-at-arms captured amounted to 4,620, these captives also losing all their equipment in addition to the ransom they would have to pay for their freedom. Also taken were 3,284 'ransom-worthy' country folk and Veronese citizens, the valueless being set free as considered nothing more than a burden. Similarly captured were the three multi-barrelled artillery carts, despite all expectations unable to fire one shot in the course of the battle. Eighty of Della Scala's senior and junior commanders fell into Paduan hands, a quarter of them German. We have these numbers thanks to Galeazzo Gatari, to which his son Andrea would add among the captured *matériel*: 384 wagons and carts loaded with bread and wine; 40 carts of lead-tipped maces; 24 large and small bombards; 20 wagons loaded with equipment for building bridges, field fortifications and siege works. Twice in less than nine months Antonio Della Scala had received a crippling military and financial blow. Would the Venetians come to his aid again?

The courier with Francesco Novello's message reached Padua at dawn on 12 March and was immediately admitted to the elder Carrara's presence. Francesco il Vecchio initially suspected bad news, not having received any from the army for some days, and joyfully relieved when the courier announced the great victory and showed Francesco Novello's damaged jupon as evidence of his bravery. After questioning him closely about the details surrounding the battle and enquiring about his commander's health, the ruling lord of Padua heard that the prisoners' ransom would cover his army's expenses. 'This is of the least importance. May God gives us every hour such victories', he exclaimed with a smile and immediately ordered prayers of thanksgiving to the Almighty. He also made preparations for his son's triumphal entry into the city, 'in the custom of the ancient Romans'.

Somebody else would also be rejoicing soon. Once he learned of the battle's outcome, Gian Galeazzo Visconti decided that the time had come to reap the fruits of his manipulative politics. In his Milanese parlour the spider, the Count of Virtue, awaited a triumph of his own.

THE AFTERMATH

Francesco Novello heard of the planned festivities while riding to Padua at the head of his victorious army. Another courier was dispatched with the younger Carrara's request that no triumph should be held: he had won only thanks to God's help and the efforts of Hawkwood, Ubaldini and the other Paduan commanders. Francesco Novello was fair-minded enough to recognize that the battle had been won not because of, but despite his own actions. Francesco il Vecchio resigned himself to his son's wishes, but nonetheless intended to have some sort of celebration for the victory. When Francesco Novello reached Padua on 15 March he found his father and the court waiting for him outside the Pontecorvo gate. Father and son embraced each other and then Francesco il Vecchio turned to Ordelaffi and Polenta, saying: 'Welcome, I see you again with pleasure', he having not seen the two Veronese condottieri since they had been ransomed in the aftermath of the battle of the Brentelle. 'We can't say the same', retorted Ordelaffi in bitterness, 'but God's will be done'. The victorious army paraded through the city displaying the captured booty and banners, the citizenry shouting 'Carro, Carro!' Francesco il Vecchio then invited his captains and the prisoners of rank to a sumptuous banquet. In a show of magnanimity, he also freed the seriously wounded Veronese peasants; although the fact that he did not wish to saddle himself with the cost of their medical care appears somewhat less generous.

Despite the successes in the war, the Carrara regime was in dire financial straits. The conflict had been extremely costly, and Antonio Della Scala was already planning to rebuild his army with Venetian money. Consequently, on the morrow of Castagnaro, Francesco il Vecchio sent an embassy to Milan to negotiate a league with Gian Galeazzo Visconti against Verona. The Count of Virtue jumped at the juicy opportunity, agreeing to negotiate a military alliance with the proviso that, should matters develop accordingly, the Veronese state would be divided between the confederates, Gian Galeazzo receiving Verona, and Vicenza going to Francesco il Vecchio. Milan would also finance the war effort. In a rush to finish Della Scala for good, the elder Carrara was but another fly unwittingly walking into the Milanese spider's parlour.

Alarmed by the military developments in northern Italy and not wishing to see the political balance there altered, the Holy Roman Emperor-Elect Wenceslaus IV sent two diplomats to Padua in an attempt to broker a peace between Carrara and Della Scala. Francesco il Vecchio answered the ambassadors' peace proposals by accusing his Veronese counterpart of

Once the castle of Ezzelino III da Romano, whose feud with Jacopo da Carrara in the 13th century sparked the Veronese-Paduan wars that were fought for more than one and a half centuries, Soave Castle became a possession of the city of Verona in 1270. Refortified by the Della Scalas only eight years before Castagnaro, it became a valued prize of Padua following the battle, only to fall to Venice in 1405. (Author's Collection)

insincerity and treachery; nevertheless, he agreed to a peace conference. Della Scala initially showed himself willing to negotiate, but objected to holding the diplomatic meeting on Paduan territory; he then killed any possible deal by stating that he could not agree to any treaty without the approval of Venice and his allies in Friuli. In the meantime, Gian Galeazzo had been urging Francesco il Vecchio not to reach an agreement with Della Scala, hinting that otherwise he could switch partners and form an alliance with Verona. Veronese obstinacy and Paduan territorial ambitions made such threats useless and the league between Milan and Padua was signed on 17 April, Mantua a third signatory.

Military operations resumed immediately. But although Ubaldini, now in Milanese pay with Francesco il Vecchio's blessing, obtained some success, the Paduan army under Francesco Novello was able to conduct a few, limited raids. Part of the problem lay in the rising tension between the younger Carrara and Hawkwood, the English captain ever more annoyed by Francesco Novello's continued disregard for his advice and instructions. The rift between the two men grew so deep that Francesco il Vecchio seriously considered having Sir John executed, the Florentine government forced to intervene to save his head. At the end of April, Hawkwood, his contract with Padua having expired, returned to Florence with his company, his place taken by a less talented, if cheaper *condottiere*.

The Milanese-Paduan offensive against Della Scala picked up speed in the spring, Visconti's troops taking several Veronese fortresses on Lake Garda while Ubaldini ravaged the land around Verona. At the beginning of June, the Paduans under Francesco Novello tried to storm Vicenza, only to be repulsed by the defenders; they made up for the reverse by taking the nearby stronghold of Montegalda at the end of July. In the Friuli, Facino Cane carried all in front of him and Francesco Novello obtained Sacile in mid-September. All these operations were conceived with the objective of preventing the Veronese troops gathering in Mestre from reaching Verona and at the same time keeping the Venetians occupied in the Friuli. Venice was also embroiled in a struggle with the kingdom of Hungary over the control of Dalmatia and thus not in a position to help its ally to the west.

Sensing the noose tightening, having no external aid in sight and domestic dissent increasing by the day, Antonio Della Scala made a last-ditch attempt to thwart his enemies by offering Verona and Vicenza to the Emperor-elect on condition he be made imperial vicar for the two cities.

An embassy from Wenceslaus was duly dispatched to bring the opposing parties together. Visconti, while openly favourable to the initiative, in secret communicated to Francesco il Vecchio not to accept any agreement, since soon the two would be carving up Della Scala's domains between themselves. By now the Count of Virtue had Verona in his grasp, already having allies within the city. On the night of 18 October, the San Massimo gate was stormed and taken by Ubaldini, thanks also to a group of its defenders switching sides. All support crumbling and his men deserting, Della Scala realized the game was up. The next day he fled Verona with his family after entrusting the city to the Imperial delegates, who, faced with a fait accompli, promptly handed it over to Visconti's representatives. The unfortunate Antonio would die the following year, still nourishing hopes to retake his native city.

With Verona in his hands, the Count of Virtue showed his true colours. Immediately after the fall of Verona, Milanese troops under Ugolotto Biancardo – now in Gian Galeazzo's pay – obtained the submission of Vicenza, refusing steadfastly to hand it over to the Paduans. In the face of Francesco il Vecchio's protests, Visconti delayed by putting forward a flurry of excuses for not delivering the city, while at the same time swearing he intended to honour his commitments to Carrara. Like a skilled chess player, Gian Galeazzo was already several moves ahead of his opponents. In December he sabotaged the peace talks between Padua, Udine and Venice over the war in Friuli; he then started provoking Francesco il Vecchio with spurious territorial and legal requests. Finally, at the end of May 1388, Milan, Venice, Mantua and even Ferrara united in a league against Padua.

Francesco il Vecchio found himself isolated: the Patriarch of Aquileia Philippe d'Alençon had been forced by increasing difficulties to renounce his see, thus depriving Carrara of his main supporter in Friuli; Florence, ostensibly Padua's ally, was in no position to intervene, owing to its military unpreparedness; Carrara's own subjects were restless, tired of years of war, destruction and oppressive taxation. Recognizing himself to be a substantial part of the problem, Francesco il Vecchio tried to forestall the inevitable by passing the reins of power and all his property to Francesco Novello at the end of June. All this proved useless. Ignoring the change of leadership in Padua, during the summer the allied forces took stronghold after stronghold, often the inhabitants opening their gates to the invaders. By mid-November, Francesco Novello was reduced to just Padua, under siege and facing a rebellious citizenry. A week later he surrendered on condition of retaining for himself the citadel until a peace settlement had been reached. This proved little more than a political fig leaf and on 11 February 1389 he formally ceded all his remaining possessions to Gian Galeazzo. Venice's spoils of war included Treviso and a free hand in Friuli.

Just after Castagnaro, Francesco il Vecchio had written to Antonio Della Scala reminding him of Aesop's fable about the frog killing a mouse by luring it to the water, the rodent being then snatched by a hawk while still attached to the amphibian and both ending up eaten. The message was clear: unless we come to an agreement, we shall both be swallowed by some other bigger state. It is therefore ironic that the older Carrara had gone on to play frog to Della Scala's mouse, in an environment such as Italy, where hawks abounded.

THE BATTLEFIELD TODAY

To reach Castagnaro by train, the best option is to travel from Verona, if coming from the north, or from Rovigo, from the south. Trains for Castagnaro run fairly regularly: roughly once every hour from Verona and every two from Rovigo. Once in Castagnaro it is about a 3km walk to the battlefield going east. Some of the way is on dirt roads, so remember to take hardy hiking footwear. By car, you just take the SS 434, running south from Verona and north from Rovigo, turn at Villa d'Adige and continue to the road running atop the levee on the Adige River. The battlefield will be to the west from there.

The rise provided by the levee allows for the best view, even if the landscape has changed significantly since 1387: gone are the Castagnaro canal and the marsh created by it, while the urban sprawl of the towns of Castagnaro and Villa d'Adige have encroached on the once-bare terrain. Many features of the battle are still present, however; and, even if we do not know the exact position of the Paduan-held ditch, the existing

Most of the battlefield where the battle of Brentelle was fought in 1386 has been built over by suburban development in the years since the Middle Ages. A visit to the Commonwealth War Graves Cemetery, which holds the remains of World War II soldiers, nevertheless provides an idea of the terrain on which the battle was fought. (Author's Collection)

channels give us a good idea how the Carrara array might have appeared to the Veronese coming from the north. Likewise, even if the course of the Adige has changed, the levee follows its original turns, as verified by recent geothermic surveys. Thus, Hawkwood's flanking charge is easily imaginable from the high ground, even if the missing swamp does not allow us to appreciate in full its effect on the Veronese line. The *bastida* present at the time of the battle has long since vanished and no traces of it remain.

The battlefield at the Brentelle has been largely obliterated by Padua's suburban expansion, only the area around the Commonwealth War Graves Cemetery being still open. Besides, many of the buildings immediately outside the city walls, present at the time of the battle, were demolished in 1509, at

A walk along the levee next to the Adige River provides an excellent view of the battlefield of Castagnaro. From here the ditch behind which his right flank was positioned can be seen (to the left of this picture), as can the battlefield where the Veronese were pushed to a diagonal advance by the longbow shot raining down on them from archers positioned roughly where this photo was taken. (Author's Collection)

Further along the levee the original position of the Veronese left flank can be seen (approximately where the ploughed field ends at the line of trees). The standards captured by Hawkwood's race behind the advancing Veronese troops would have been in the distance, perhaps in the field near the building in the centre of this photograph. (Author's Collection)

Montagnana's medieval walls have existed since three centuries before the time of the battle of Castagnaro. While some elements may be exaggerated – the crenelations are far too large, for example – those visiting the town today can witness the strength of well built and maintained medieval fortifications. (Author's Collection)

the time of the war of the League of Cambrai, when Padua came under siege from Maximilian I of Habsburg's troops. The roads existing at the time of the Brentelle battle are still identifiable, though, and one can imagine the routed Paduan militia fleeing down the present-day Via Chiesanuova towards the Savonarola city gate.

Much more rewarding is following the campaign trails of the various armies. You'll need a car for that, but a chance to behold the once-Veronese or Paduan fortified towns of the area is well worth the effort. Monselice, Montagnana, Marostica and many of the other settlements mentioned in the text make for some very memorable visits; in particular if one should wish to combine the historical with the artistic and the oenological – the wines of the Veneto and the Friuli are famous worldwide and a pleasant relief after a day passed delving into the past.

BIBLIOGRAPHY

Primary Sources

Cipolla, Carlo, ed., *Antiche cronache veronesi*, Venice: Deputazione veneta di Storia patria, 1890

Chronicon Estense, cum additamentis usque ad annum 1478, Giulio Bertoni and Emilio Paolo Vicini, ed., in *Rerum Italicarum Scriptores II*, vol. 15, part 3, Città di Castello: Lapi, 1908

Codex Diplomaticus Dominii Temporalis S. Sedis, Augustin Theiner, ed., vol. 2: 1335–1389, Rome: Stamperia Vaticana, 1862

Conforto da Costoza, *Frammenti di Storia vicentina (1371–1387)*, Carlo Steiner, ed., in *Rerum Italicarum Scriptores II*, vol. 13, part 1, Città di Castello: Lapi 1915

Cronica volgare di anonimo fiorentino: dall'anno 1385 al 1409; già attribuita a Piero di Giovanni Minerbetti, Elina Bellondi, ed., in *Rerum Italicarum Scriptores II*, vol. 27, part 2, Città di Castello: Lapi, 1915–1918

Diario d'anonimo fiorentino dal 1358 al 1389, Alessandro Gherardi, ed., in *Cronache dei secoli XIII e XIV*, Florence: Cellini, 1876

Gatari, Galeazzo e Bartolomeo, *Cronaca carrarese: confrontata con la redazione di Andrea Gatari: aa. 1318–1407*, Antonio Medin and Guido Tolomei, ed., in *Rerum Italicarum Scriptores II*, vol. 17, part 1, section 1, Città di Castello: Lapi, 1909–1931

Gesta magnifica domus Carrariensis, Roberto Cessi, ed., in *Rerum Italicarum Scriptores II*, vol. 17, part 1, section 3, Bologna: Zanichelli, 1965

Livingston, Michael and DeVries, Kelly, ed., *The Battle of Crécy: A Casebook*, Liverpool: Liverpool University Press, 2015

Ludovico Antonio Muratori ed., in *Rerum Italicarum Scriptores*, vol. 19, Milan: Società Palatina, 1731

Paride da Cerea, *Il Chronicon Veronense di Paride da Cerea e dei suoi continuatori*, Renzo Vaccari, ed., vol. 3, Legnago: Fondazione Fioroni, 2014

Redusi, Andrea, *Chronicon tarvisinum ab anno MCCCLXVIII usque ad annum MCCCCXXVII*,

Sacchetti, Franco, *Tales From Sacchetti*, Mary G. Steegman trans., London: J. M. Dent & Co., 1908

Secondary Sources

Bueno de Mesquita, Daniel M., *Giangaleazzo Visconti, Duke of Milan (1351–1402)*, Cambridge, Mass.: Harvard University Press, 1941

Caferro, William, *John Hawkwood: An English Mercenary in Fourteenth-Century Italy*, Baltimore: The Johns Hopkins University Press, 2006

———, 'Mercenaries and Military Expenditure: The Costs of Undeclared Warfare in Fourteenth Century Siena' in *Journal of European Economic History* 23 (1994): 219–247

Capasso, Carlo, 'I provvisionati di Bernabò Visconti' in *Archivio Storico Lombardo*, 4th ser., 15 (1911): 285–304

Carli, Alessandro, *Istoria Della città di Verona sino all'anno 1517: divisa in undici epoche*, vol. 5, Venice: Stamperia Giuliani, 1796

Castagnetti, Andrea, and Varanini, Gian Maria, eds., *Il Veneto nel medioevo: Le signorie trecentesche*, Verona: Banca popolare di Verona, 1995

Cessi, Roberto, 'Prigionieri illustri durante la guerra fra Scaligeri e Carraresi (1386)' in *Atti Della Reale. Accademia delle scienze di Torino*, 40 (1904–1905): 976–994

CittaDella, Giovanni, *Storia Della Dominazione Carrarese in Padova*, 2 vol., Padua: Tipi del Seminario, 1842

Collino, Giovanni, 'La guerra Viscontea contro gli Scaligeri nelle relazioni diplomatiche fiorentine- bolognesi col conte di Virtù (1386–1387)' in *Archivio Storico Lombardo* 34 (1907): 105–159

De Marco, Enzo, 'Crepuscolo degli Scaligeri (La Signoria di Antonio Della Scala): 12 luglio 1381–18 ottobre 1387' in *Archivio Veneto*, 5th ser., 68–69 (1938-1939): 107–206, 1–120

De Stefani, Giuseppe, *Bartolomeo ed Antonio Dalla Scala. Saggio storico*, Verona: Drucker e Tedeschi, 1884

Durrieu, Paul, 'La prise d'Arezzo par Enguerrand VII, sire de Coucy en 1384' in *Bibliothèque de l'École des Chartres* 41 (1880): 161–194

Fowler, Kenneth, 'Sir John Hawkwood and the English Condottieri in Trecento Italy' in *Renaissance Studies* 11 (1998): 131–148

Hall, Bert S., *Weapons and Warfare in Renaissance Europe*, Baltimore: Johns Hopkins University Press, 1997

Kohl, Benjamin G., *Padua Under the Carrara, 1318–1405*, Baltimore: Johns Hopkins University Press, 1998

Law, John E., 'La caduta degli Scaligeri' in *Istituzioni, societa e potere nella Marca Trivigiana e Veronese, secoli XIII–XIV*, ed. Ortalli, Gherardo and Knapton, Michael, Rome: Istituto storico italiano per il Medio Evo, 1988: 83–98

Mallett, Michael E., *Mercenaries and Their Masters: Warfare in Renaissance Italy*, Lanham: Rowman and Littlefield, 1974

Novati, Francesco, 'Trattive di Giangaleazzo Visconti con condottieri di ventura durante la guerra contro Antonio Della Scala (1387)' in *Archivio Storico Lombardo* 39 (1912): 572–577

Ricotti, Ercole, *Storia delle compagnie di ventura in Italia*, vol. 1–2, Turin: Pomba, 1844

Selzer, Stephan, *Deutsche Söldner Im Italien des Trecento*, Tübingen: Niemeyer Max Verlag GmbH, 2001

Settia, Aldo A., *Comuni in guerra: Armi ed eserciti nell'Italia delle città*, Bologna: Clueb, 1993

Temple-Leader, John, and Marcotti, Giuseppe, *Sir John Hawkwood (L'Acuto): Story of a Condottiere*, Leader Scott trans., London: T. Fisher Unwin, 1889

Varanini, Gian Maria, ed., *Gli Scaligeri 1277–1387*, Milan: Mondadori, 1988

Varanini, Gian Maria and Bianchi, Francesco, eds., *La guerra scaligero-veronese e la battaglia del Castagnaro (1387)*, Vicenza: Istituto per le ricerche di storia sociale e religiosa, 2015

Verci, Giambattista, *Storia Della marca trivigiana e veronese*, voll. 15–16, Venice: Giacomo Storti, 1790

INDEX